MW01602584

Wildlife Conservation and Tourism in Kenya

Daniel Musili Nyeki

Senior Education Officer
Kenya Wildlife Service.

*A percentage of the sale proceeds of this book
will be donated to the Kenya Wildlife Service
in support of conservation projects.*

Published by Jacaranda Designs, Ltd. P.O.Box 76691 Nairobi, Kenya
Copyright (c) Jacaranda Designs, Ltd.
First Published 1993.
Text by Daniel M. Nyeki. Edited by Bridget King.
Cover Design by Ladan Doorandish-Vance.
Cartoons by S. Echaria. Illustrations by P. Kanyare and S. Ngoje.
Photographs by Fineline Media, Bridget King, V. Taylor and KWS

ISBN 9966-884-96-3

Typeset in Palatino
Colour separations by EnColour. Printed by Autolitho, Ltd.
Produced *entirely* in Kenya.

Table of Contents

KENYA WILDLIFE SERVICE

FOREWORD

This year marks the first international Earth Summit convened to underscore the critical role a healthy and well-managed environment has in the growth and prosperity of all human, animal and plant life. The state of our people, our wildlife, natural environment and our life sustaining eco-systems have never before been at such risk; and never before have we, the people, been called upon to care so much.

In Kenya, the need for information and education about our wildlife and natural conservation is so important. The necessity to preserve our rich natural heritage cannot be over-emphasized; it is paramount to the economic and environmental well-being of our nation.

Produced for students and visitors to Kenya, this book is compiled from a manuscript developed by our Senior Education Officer, Mr. Daniel Nyeki. I hope this well-researched and up to date book will guide the youth of Kenya to give serious attention to their present and future roles in the maintenance of a healthy environment. And, I also hope this book will help Kenyans and our visitors more fully to appreciate the work being done to protect this valued resource by the Kenya Wildlife Service for the present and future enjoyment of all.

Dr. Richard Leakey
Director of Kenya Wildlife Service

Acknowledgements

Many people have contributed their knowledge and expertise to make this book as up to date and as accurate as possible. To all of them I would extend my deepest appreciation. In particular I would like to mention: Ms. Judith Rudnai who contributed important notes on the ecology, conservation and management of wild animals, most of which were incorporated into this book. I also wish to gratefully acknowledge Simon Gitau and Judith Ochilo who assisted in drawing up the general outline of the book. Mr. Steve Meacher of the World Society for the Protection of Animals, Dr. Chris Gakahu of Wildlife Conservation International, Dr. Esmond Martin of World Wildlife Fund for Nature and Mr. Nathan Munyori of Abercrombie & Kent who all spent precious time reading the manuscript and giving valuable advice. Special thanks are also due to Dr. Joyce Poole and Dr. Rob Brett of K.W.S., Dr. Iain Douglas-Hamilton, and Bridget King for the overall editing of the manuscript with layout assistance from Susan Scull-Carvalho.

Daniel Musili Nyeki
Senior Education Officer
Kenya Wildlife Service

INTRODUCTION

What is environmental conservation?

Many people wonder why the radio, television and newspapers are full of talk about environmental conservation today. Why did the Kenyan Government ban hunting in 1977? Why did President Daniel arap Moi demonstrate to the world the evils of trade in game trophies by burning to ashes 12 tons of ivory in 1989? Why have governments throughout the world banned the importation and selling of animal skins, tusks and horns as well as live animals? Why do governments try to stop the cutting and burning of indigenous trees and the tropical rainforests?

People everywhere discuss the need to protect the remaining species of wild animals and birds from extinction, but why is there so much concern?

Global village

Scientists throughout the world have discovered that our world is like a large village and what we do in one part of the world affects people living in another part. For example if one country produces a large amount of carbon dioxide and other poisonous fumes from their factories, then it will affect the air in another country and the rain will become acid. This in turn will damage the trees and vegetation. If people living near the source of a river pour human waste and chemicals from their factories into the rivers then not only will they kill off the fish and plants in that river but the people downstream will also be affected. When the river finally runs into the sea, the marine life is also poisoned by the chemicals. Humans then catch and eat the fish and so absorb more poisonous chemicals into their bodies which can cause illness and even death.

i

The environment

The air we breathe, the waters which cover two-thirds of the world, and the earth in which we grow our crops all form our environment. It is our environment which keeps us and other living things alive . Whatever we do that damages the environment affects the health of all other living things, plants and animals as well as ourselves.

Conservation of the environment

Conservation is the control of human use of the living and non-living resources. We must control the way humans use the living resources (plants and animals) and non-living resources (air, water, soil and minerals). If we conserve the environment we will benefit both present and futures generations. If we do not do this, the results will be disastrous.

Kenya's role in conservation

How does conservation involve Kenya? Kenya still has much undeveloped land which is not used for either agriculture or human habitation. Forests and water bodies play an important role in the water cycle as they affect the rainfall, which in turn affects agriculture.

Within the unpopulated areas of Kenya live hundreds of different species of animals (fauna) and plants (flora). Some of these species of flora and fauna can be found nowhere else in the world. They attract visitors from outside Kenya who come to see and study them. Kenya welcomes over 800,000 visitors a year and it is these visitors who have brought about a new industry in the country, namely tourism.

Tourism

There are several different kinds of tourists who come to Kenya to see the wild animals, the beautiful scenery and to relax on the beaches. There are the true tourists who come only for pleasure and recreation; there are the business people who also visit tourist places for pleasure and recreation; and there are local (domestic) tourists who visit other parts of the country for recreational purposes.

Tourism is now an important industry for Kenya bringing in Ksh 11.9 billion each year. As well as the direct income, tourism also helps to create direct and indirect employment for thousands of Kenyans as well as creating markets for agricultural produce. If the natural resources did not exist, tourists would not be attracted to this country in such large numbers and the benefits would not be so great.

CHAPTER I

The Beginnings of Conservation

Since ancient times human beings have practised conservation although they did not think of it in those terms. The Stone-Age hunters and gatherers, for example, hunted only a limited number of the wild animals for their daily subsistence. They killed only mature (fully grown) healthy animals but left the young ones and potential mothers unharmed. They only hunted certain species of animals for their food. Those animals which were believed to be sacred, or those which were considered taboo, were left unharmed, to avoid misfortune such as death and disease attacking the community. Certain trees or shrubs were not cut or destroyed because they were used as shrines for prayers, or their bark, roots and leaves were kept for medicinal purposes. These practices ensured the growth, prosperity and survival of the wild animal and plant species.

In this way people co-existed or lived harmoniously with their environment. This kind of co-existence without destruction was possible at a time when:

- The human population was small compared to the available resource such as land, plants and animals;

- Land use practices did not change dramatically, for example there was no need for large farms or ranches to raise food and no large areas were set aside for settlement, road construction, timber harvesting or other development;

- The available resources were not exploited for commercial gain, e.g. hunting for skins, tusks and horn (game trophies) or meat for sale.

In more modern times, ancient hunting grounds, particularly in Europe and North America, were kept for the privileged few. Only rulers and noblemen were allowed to hunt in these areas; in this way hunting was very limited.

However today these areas are open and accessible to everybody. So how is hunting controlled? Hunters have to buy licences which allow them to shoot a limited number of animals and they may do so only during certain seasons. In this way, the number of animals killed is strictly controlled and over-exploitation prevented.

New concept of conservation
During the past hundred years or so, a new concept of conservation has developed. It began with a group of explorers at the historic campfire in Yellowstone, USA in 1870. They decided that the area had such natural beauty that it should be made a *"public park or pleasuring ground for the benefit and enjoyment of the people"*. Two years later the government passed a bill authorizing such use, and the words "National Park" came into official use.

Many other countries followed this example: Canada protected the area around the mineral hot springs at Banff in 1885 which later became Banff National Park; the National Trust of Great Britain was founded in 1895 to conserve places of national interest; the Laponia National Reserve in Sweden was established in 1909. The first game reserve on the African continent was created by President Kruger of South Africa in 1892. This was called Sabi Game Reserve, which later became the world famous Kruger National Park.

Later the London Conference for the Protection of African Fauna and Flora encouraged the creation of nature reserves and national parks on this continent. The Bukavu Conference of 1953 officially recognised the great national parks of East and Central Africa.

In the last fifty years, the Kenya Government has shown its dedication to the conservation of wildlife and natural environment by establishing a large number of protected areas.

The development of Kenya's conservation legislation
At the time when the Kenya-Uganda railway was being built, the area now known as Tsavo National Park was full of wild animals (game) of all descriptions. This was because most pastoral tribes, such as the Maasai, felt that game meat was inferior to their traditional meat (cows, sheep and goats) and they would not kill wild animals unless the animals interfered with their livestock. The few tribes who did hunt wild animals for meat used simple weapons and killed only those animals which they needed for their daily

2

sustenance. Land cultivations were small and there was therefore enough room for the game and humans to co-exist in harmony.

At the end of the 19th century,the enormous decrease in the human population through plague, smallpox and sleeping sickness left large areas of land free for wild animals. The wildlife populations increased to such an extent that one traveller through Maasailand described herds of gazelles stretching for as far as the eye could see. Early in the 20th century, the country became a paradise for hunters who arrived in large numbers with fast vehicles, firearms and overseas buyers greedy for game trophies.

The resulting hunting pressure and decrease in wildlife populations caused the authorities to call the first ever international conference on wildlife conservation and management. As a result of the meeting the regional authorities passed the first laws for game conservation in Kenya. The East African Game Regulations of 1900 were strengthened by the game ordinance (rules) and amendments in 1904, 1905 and 1906. Finally in 1907 the government created the Kenya Game Department. Later the Game Ordinance of 1909, a very comprehensive document, became a law. Under this ordinance the government proclaimed the southern Game Reserve in Maasailand and the Northern Game Reserve in the Northern Frontier Province.

For a decade after that there was no legislation on the game laws, but the 1920's and 1930's saw further advanced reforms: for example the authorities declared a ban on hunting certain species of animals during certain seasons; the Southern Game Reserve was expanded to include part of the future Tsavo West National Park; the Game Birds Protection Ordinance of 1926 greatly improved the East African Wild Bird Protection Ordinance of 1903.

The second International Conference on Wildlife Conservation was held in London late in 1933. The participants generally agreed on the principle of establishing and maintaining national parks or permanent wildlife sanctuaries in East Africa. Subsequently, an ordinance was passed in 1937 to strengthen and improve the law relating to the protection of game animals and birds in Kenya. On the basis of this, the government appointed the Game Policy Committee in 1938 to recommend where and how to establish a system of national parks. World War Two delayed the work but the committee produced a report and on the basis of this report, Ordinance No.9 of 1945 was established. Under the ordinance, a Board of Trustees was appointed to administer the areas of land designated as national parks and national reserves for *"the preservation of wild flora and fauna and objects of aesthetic (beauty), geological, prehistoric, historical, archaeological or scientific interest"*. This was cited as the National Parks Ordinance, through which Nairobi National Park was established by proclamation on 16th December, 1946 and Tsavo National Park in April, 1948.

The Ordinance was changed to the Royal National Parks of Kenya Ordinance (later to be known as the National Parks of Kenya Act). Under the ordinance Mt. Kenya National Park was established in 1949, Aberdares National Park in 1950, Marsabit National Reserve in 1962, Mt. Elgon National Park in 1968, Lake Nakuru National Park in 1967, Meru National Park in 1966, Shimba Hills National Reserve in 1968, Malindi/Watamu Marine National Parks in 1968, Sibiloi National Park in 1973 and Amboseli National Park in 1974. Other National Parks and Reserves were established later, giving Kenya 26 National Parks, 29 National Reserves and one Game Sanctuary by the end of 1991. This brings the total protected wildlife conservation area to 44,720 square kilometers or 7.7% of the total area of Kenya.

Government Conservation Institutions

After the 1945 changes, two government institutions administered wildlife in Kenya: The Kenya National Parks Organization and the Game Department.

> **The Kenya National Parks Organization** administered the national parks and national reserves. It protected those areas as wildlife preservation sanctuaries. At the same time it developed them as tourist resorts or pleasure grounds for the benefit and enjoyment of the general public.

> **The Game Department** administered and controlled all wild animals outside the authority of the national parks, including those on private land. It established District Game Stations in areas where wildlife was an important resource. In addition the Department advised and assisted local county councils to establish their Game Reserves where hunting of wild animals was forbidden. The rest of the wildlife areas under the various county councils were officially declared hunting blocks where licensed hunting was allowed under the control of the Department.

> To encourage the local people to understand and appreciate the need for wildlife conservation, and to develop good relations between the Department and the local people, the Game Depart-

4

ment gave financial help (in the form of grants) to local authorities. These grants were for the construction and the development of public utilities such as primary schools, dispensaries and cattle dips. The councils also used the grants to pay compensation for loss of life or property caused by wildlife.

In 1976 an act of Parliament merged the two wildlife conservation organizations into one government department, the **Wildlife Conservation and Management Department,** under the Ministry of Tourism and Wildlife. The new department brought together all matters concerning wildlife conservation in the country and became the only overall wildlife authority, on stateland, trustland or private land. It was responsible for conserving and managing all wildlife in the country and to ensure that the resource gave back the best possible returns to individuals and the nation in terms of cultural, aesthetic and economic gains. Such utilization was to be carried out in a way that would not be harmful to conservation principles.

However, licensed hunting and poaching continued to destroy wildlife on a large scale. This situation forced the government in May 1977 to ban all hunting of wild animals and the handling of and trading in game trophies. The ban caused the closure of the professional hunting companies and curio shops which dealt in game trophies but did not solve the poaching problem which continued unchecked. Poaching seriously reduced the population of certain animal species, especially the elephant and rhino. It was so bad that towards the end of 1987 a change in conservation and management policy was essential if Kenya was to save her remaining stock of her valuable wild animals.

Consequently, the Wildlife Conservation and Management Act was amended to create the **Kenya Wildlife Service (KWS).** KWS is a state corporation which is largely self-governing. It has been given the responsibility of conserving the Kenyan natural environment and its fauna and flora. This is done for the benefit of the present and future generations both in Kenya and the world. It is also responsible for

The logo of Kenya Wildlife Service

5

utilizing the wildlife resources of Kenya sustainably for her national economic development and for the benefit of the people living in wildlife areas. At the same time the corporation is responsible for protecting the people and their property from damage by wildlife.

The corporation started operations in July 1989 and was officially launched in January 1990. Under the amended Act the corporation is allowed to use its financial resources and powers as it considers appropriate. In this way it is able to respond quickly and effectively to the demands of wildlife protection and management throughout the country. It also raises financial, material and other assistance from both local and international sources.

The amended Act empowers the Minister responsible for wildlife conservation and management to appoint a Board of Trustees to run KWS. The Trustees, under a Chairman, make policies and regulations for the protection and management of wildlife and national parks in Kenya. These have to be approved and published in the Kenya Gazette by the Minister before they become law. The Board has powers to declare, establish, de-gazette or close National Parks/Reserves and Game Sanctuaries. The Board can change Park/Reserve boundaries, adjust mining regulations and entry fees and determine hunting policy. They have the power to dispose of game trophies, to control the export of live animals, and to protect endangered species.

The Service Director (the Secretary and the Executive Officer of the Board) has general control of all wildlife affairs in the country. Through his field officers, the Director protects and manages all wildlife and conservation areas, controls the operations of the service, appoints honorary game wardens, controls commercial operations and the capture and translocation (removal to another place) of wild animals. The Director also issues utilization licences and consults the local authorities and communities about the conservation and management of wildlife in their areas.

In 1992 KWS inaugurated a Community Conservation Department. This department ensures the participation of the communities living adjacent to the conservation areas and involves them in the day to day running of the conservation areas. It also gives back some of the financial benefits accruing from wildlife conservation to the local communities. This is given directly or through the construction of community utilities such as schools, dispensaries, cattle dips, water supplies, etc. as a way of revenue sharing. In this way, wildlife and human conflicts are minimised and the communities are mobilized to participate in sustainable wildlife conservation and utilization programmes for their own economic gains.

In the National Parks and Reserves, KWS has managed to effectively conserve Kenya's natural resources in order to provide high quality natural environments for the recreational enjoyment of the tourists. High standard facilities such as lodges, roads, airstrips, campsites, picnic sites and game observation points have ben established.

Anti-poaching

The KWS organisation has acquired a large amount of equipment and finance, and now maintains a strong anti-poaching unit equipped with modern weapons, vehicles, radios and communications equipment for quick, efficient operations in the bush. The anti-poaching unit has seven base stations in important wildlife areas with mobile sections and sub-sections. These stations monitor the movement and welfare of all wild animals, particularly the elephant and rhino, the two species most hunted by commercial poachers. An efficient investigation team operates in cities, towns and rural areas to trap poachers, would-be poachers or business-men involved in the illegal trading in game trophies. It has now become almost impossible for poachers to operate in the bush or towns without being noticed by KWS agents.

President Daniel Arap Moi setting light to raw ivory in 1989

Protection of the elephant and rhino

The world-wide campaign to ban the trade in ivory has helped to ensure the survival of the elephant. On 18th July, 1989, Kenya's President Daniel Arap Moi was watched by the world as he burnt to ashes 12 metric tons of raw ivory (worth Ksh 60 million). This resulted in a complete change of attitude in the western world towards the ivory trade and the wearing of ivory jewellery. At the CITES Lausanne Conference in October 1989, Kenya led the campaign to stop the international trade in ivory. At the end of the debate, Kenya and her supporters were victorious and the international ivory trade was banned throughout the world. However, some countries not bound by this Convention continue to trade in small quantities of ivory.

Rhino sanctuaries have been established within Nairobi, Nakuru, Tsavo West and Aberdares National Parks and private rhino sanctuaries exist in the Laikipia District. Threatened rhinos are captured and transferred to the sanctuaries where they are given 24-hour protection. Rhinos are also translocated to facilitate the exchange of genetic material (inherited characteristics) and to prevent inbreeding. The rhino population is today reported to be growing at an average of 5% and the elephant population at an average of 4 - 5% a year.

Rhino being loaded onto a translocation truck

CHAPTER 2

Natural Resources Conservation

"Conservation is the control of human use of the living and non-living resources in order that they yield benefits to the present generation, while maintaining their potential to meet the needs and aspirations of future generations". In order to maintain a healthy environment, we must conserve our natural resources.

Living resources are plants and animals. Non-living resources are air, water, soil and minerals. These resources can be further classified into renewable and non-renewable categories.

Renewable resources are those which can be maintained through careful management, i.e. water, soil, plants and animals. All the things essential to our well-being, such as soil to grow our food, the water we drink, trees for timber and fuel and fodder for animals are renewable resources. Without them we would not survive.

Non-renewable resources are those which, once used, are gone forever; i.e. oil, coal, copper, gold and other minerals. The rate at which these can be replaced is so slow that it cannot compensate for our rate of use, so they will eventually become exhausted no matter how carefully utilized.
In this book we deal only with the renewable resources, particularly wildlife.

How can we conserve these vital resources? Let's look at them one at a time.

SOIL
Soil is the fine earth covering the land surface. Soil supports living plants, supplies the mineral nutrients necessary for plant growth and is the home of many animals and insects. Humans live on the soil, build on it and plant food crops in it, but unfortunately we have over-exploited this valuable resource,

causing soil erosion, pollution and loss of soil fertility.

Soil erosion

This is the removal of the fertile top soil by running water and wind. It is made worse by removing vegetation cover, by cutting down trees, burning vegetation, overgrazing the land or cultivating on hill slopes or along river banks. Soil fertility is reduced when farmers cultivate one area year after year without allowing the land to rest and regenerate or if they do not apply compost manure to the soil. The result is barren soil which cannot support either the growing vegetation or the animal life within it. This is how deserts begin.

Soil conservation

To prevent soil erosion, we should carry out soil conservation methods.

Terracing: To control the speed of running rain water which erodes the soil, we can cut terraces on hill slopes. Terraces hold much of the water for use by crops. Ploughing along the contours also helps soil conservation.

Tree Planting: If we plant trees and grasses on hill slopes, open plains and along river banks this helps to create plant cover. This vegetation cover acts like a sponge by holding moisture. It also reduces evaporation and provides a windbreak, while the roots of the plants hold the soil in position.

Proper Stocking: Farmers should keep their livestock to a number which can be supported by the available land. Too many animals cause overgrazing which leads to loss of vegetation and finally to soil erosion.

Crop Rotation: If farmers rotate their crops, they can prevent exhaustion of the soil (loss of all nutrients) and help to restore fertility. Compost, fertilizers and organic manure also add fertility to the soil and indirectly prevent soil erosion.

Building Gabions: Gabions are piles of stones, held together by wire mesh or chain link wire. They are constructed in gullies to hold back the loose soil and prevent it from being washed away. If hill slopes or river banks become badly eroded by running water, the gullies should be filled with gabions.

WATER

Water forms the basis of all life on earth. Let us look briefly at the water cycle:

Water cycle

The oceans form the main reservoirs of water on earth and are the first step in the water cycle. The energy to run the cycle comes from the heat produced by the sun. The sun's heat causes evaporation from the surface of the oceans and the resulting vapour forms clouds. The wind moves these clouds across the land which cools them. This cooling process causes precipitation in the form of rain. A lot of the rain soaks into the ground and is absorbed by plants, while more rain water runs off as surface water and finally goes back into the ocean. On its return journey, a lot of the water is taken into the bodies of several different organisms such as animals and plants.

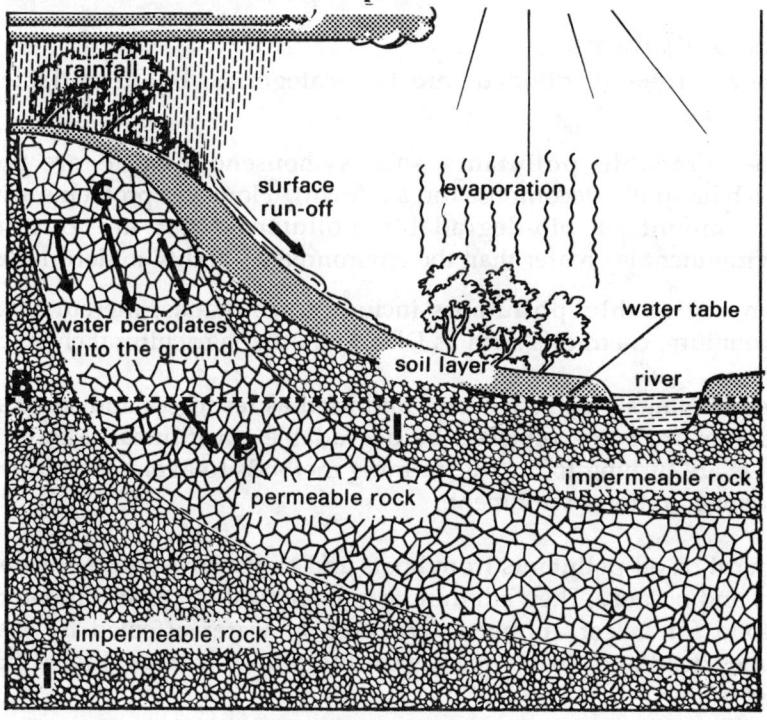

The water cycle

Water is a limiting factor for land organisms and the distribution of animals and plants in a country is governed by:

11

- the amount of rainfall in a particular area
- its seasonal distribution,
- humidity and
- supply of ground water.

Both drought and an excess of water can kill most plant and animal species.

Over-exploitation of water

People have learnt to use water in various ways to improve their standard of living: e.g. irrigation for crop production, transport, hydro-electric power, fish farming and recreation. Unfortunately, because of the increase in human population and advanced technology, we have over-exploited the water resources. This over-exploitation has resulted in pollution and other adverse effects which seriously threaten our own lives and those of other creatures.

Water Pollutants

These are roughly divided into two categories: bio-degradable and non-degradable.

Bio-degradable pollutants, such as household waste, are pollutants which naturally decompose (break down). However problems arise when the amount of bio-degradable pollutants that are put into the environment is greater than the environment's ability to decompose them.

Non-degradable pollutants include trace metals, mercury, steel and aluminium, chemicals such as DDT and other agricultural chemicals.

Some pollutants may be recycled and used as resources and some agricultural pollutants are being replaced by degradable substitutes. Many progressive farmers are turning to organic farming methods to avoid chemicals which can be a danger to the environment.

Chemical or oil pollutants from boats and ships flow into the waters of lakes, rivers and oceans. They kill minute aquatic (water) plants and animals which are food for larger animals. The area of water affected by the pollution becomes dead and unable to support life until it is rehabilitated (made fit for living in).

Chemicals can also pollute water when they are used in different stages of industrial manufacture. This happens when polluted water is often poured back into rivers, lakes or oceans without being treated or purified.

Both untreated sewage (household waste) and industrial effluent (factory waste) are sometimes allowed to flow directly into rivers, lakes or oceans or even onto open fields. This practice is dangerous to the health of the people, animals and plant life.

Oil pollutants have killed this water bird

Siltation and soil erosion

If water catchment upstream in the higher areas is damaged, soil erosion usually results. The running water sweeps the soil away depositing it further downstream where it chokes the flow of dams and rivers. This is a process known as siltation. Siltation adversely affects food production for aquatic animals in dams, lakes, rivers and oceans.

Excessive water loss is also caused by dams which have a greater surface area of water and consequently a higher rate of evaporation. Dams also create breeding habitats for water-borne carriers of disease, e.g. mosquitoes and snails. In addition dam walls may also prevent fish which breed upstream from reaching their breeding grounds.

Water Conservation

Vegetation and soil are essential for absorbing rainwater and replenishing water catchment areas. If we want to maintain a healthy water cycle, then the following controls are essential:

Terracing: Contour ploughing and planting trees and grasses on slopes which form water catchment areas will control soil erosion and help to conserve water. This will reduce surface run-off and ensure that rain water seeps slowly down through the soil. This water will either emerge as spring water or form streams and rivers.

Treatment: Any water used in industry or for the disposal of sewage must be properly treated or purified before it is allowed to flow back into rivers, lakes or oceans or recycled for direct use.

Chemicals: Farmers should carefully control the use of chemicals to stop them from seeping down through the soil where they can cause pollution to water sources.

Transportation of dangerous substances: Shipping companies should obey all the conventions and laws regarding the safe transportation of chemicals and oils across the oceans, rivers, seas and lakes. If this is done it will prevent the disastrous spilling or dumping of those pollutants in the water bodies.

AIR

Although air is essential for all life, humans have introduced poisonous gases into the atmosphere through advanced technology. These gases have endangered, and in some cases destroyed, our lives and those of other animals.

Atmospheric imbalance

The greatest danger facing us and our fellow creatures on this planet is the destruction of the natural balance of gases in the atmosphere. Since 1973, scientists working under the auspices of the United Nations Environment Programme (UNEP) have warned the world of the catastrophe which may endanger all life on earth as a result of the pollution of the earth's atmosphere and stratosphere. Some of the problems include the:

The use of Chlorofluorocarbons, known as CFCs, which are industrial gases used in refrigeration, aerosol cans, foam agents and as solvents in electronics. When these are released into the stratosphere, (the layer of atmospheric air between 10 and 60 km above the earth's surface) they destroy the ozone layer which protects the earth from harmful solar radiation.

An increase in carbon dioxide in the atmosphere as a result of the burning of fossil fuels and methane to produce power. These gases are changing the structure and balance of the atmosphere surrounding the earth. Normally, the earth's radiation escapes harmlessly into space, but these gases absorb this radiation and return more of it back to the earth. This returned energy has already increased the earth's surface temperature by 5° C since the last Ice Age and is likely to increase it further by between 1.5° C and 4.5° C by the year 2030 (UNEP Brief No.1). We call this rise in atmospheric temperature 'global warming'.

What will be the effects of global warming?

Wheat-growing areas in temperate zones of the world will shift out towards the North and South Poles. If soils in the polar zones are poor, production of wheat will fall worldwide.

Marginal agriculture in zones prone to drought, like the Sahel, will disappear, causing desertification. The result will be changes in commerce and untold human hardship.

Grasslands and deserts will expand, while forests will shrink and move towards the polar zones. This will also increase soil erosion.

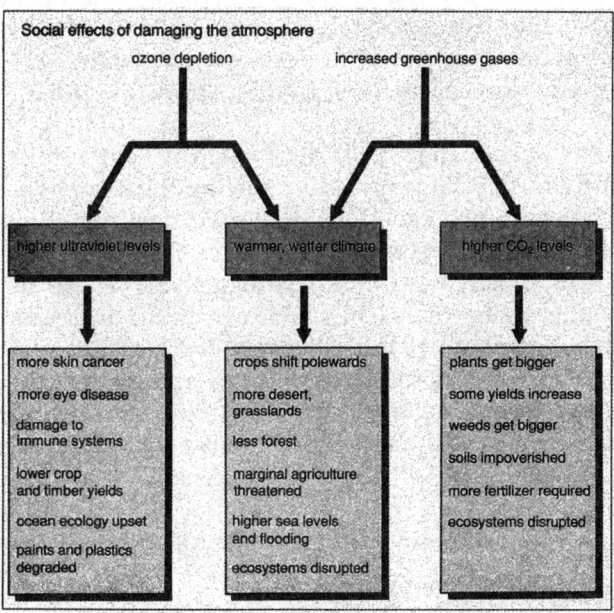

UNEP diagram showing the possible effects of global warming

Glaciers will melt and raise ocean and sea levels. This will cause widespread flooding of low-lying coastal areas.

Crops and weeds will grow faster because of increased carbon dioxide in the air, but due to a lower level of nitrogen they will be more susceptible to pests. Soils will become poorer as a result of sustaining higher rates of plant growth and farmers will therefore need more fertilizers.

Rainfall may increase by 10% due to global warming, but soils will become poorer due to increased evaporation. Increased rainfall will also affect surface water run-off, dams and reservoirs.

The Ozone Layer is found surrounding the earth at a height of 20 - 60 km, but is more dense at 20 - 25 km from the surface of the earth. Ozone is a gas composed of three oxygen atoms. It absorbs solar radiation and therefore protects life on earth from the harmful ultraviolet rays of the sun. The ozone layer almost completely absorbs the short-wave ultraviolet radiation, UV-C, which is deadly to all living things. However the longer-wave UV-A, which is relatively harmless, is allowed through. In the middle of these two lies UV-B, less lethal than UV-C but still dangerous. The ozone layer absorbs most of the UV-B, but leaves a small amount (10-30%) to reach the earth. The small amount that reaches the earth destroys the genetic material, DNA, and is the main cause of skin cancer. (Ref: UNEP: Action on Ozone).

Scientists now agree that pollution of the earth's stratosphere by chlorofluorocarbons (CFCs) is already reducing the composition and strength of the ozone layer. Since each CFC molecule destroys thousands of ozone molecules, CFCs are the major destroyers of the ozone layer. Halons are related substances, mostly used in fire extinguishers. These are ten times more destructive to the ozone than CFCs. However the increase of CFCs in the stratosphere has been shown to be the real cause of ozone destruction. For example, a hole as wide as the United States and as deep as Mount Everest has opened up in the ozone layer over Antarctica and it grows larger as the ozone layer diminishes. No-one knows for sure what all the consequences of this hole will be (UNEP).

The increase in UV-B radiation will have the following serious effects:

• Wrinkling and early ageing of the skin;

• Increased skin cancer, which already kills about 6,000 people per year in the USA;

- Increased loss of natural immunity (the body's defence against disease) and increased vulnerability to disease;

- Increased cataracts of the eyes, which already blinds 12 - 15 million people and damages the vision of another 18 to 30 million a year worldwide;

- Lower yields of some crops, e.g. peas, beans, cabbage, tomato;

- Destruction of marine life like plankton, shrimp, crab and plants which are essential to the food chain of the sea. UV-B radiation strikes beneath the surface of the sea, causing damage up to 20 metres deep;

- Damage to paints and plastics which break down and become brittle;

- Acid rain (caused by urban air pollution) will increase over cities as UV-B radiation increases.

There is evidence that the ozone layer is thinning all over the world. If we continue to release CFCs and halons into the stratosphere, the ozone layer will decrease by 20% within our children's life time. This will cause an extra 1.5 million human deaths from skin cancer and 5 million extra cataracts in the USA alone (UNEP).

The greenhouse effect: As the ozone layer decreases and allows more solar radiation through to the earth, the average temperature of the earth's surface increases. This global warming is called the greenhouse effect. The increase of CFCs and halons in the stratosphere is likely to contribute greater damage to the greenhouse effect than so far imagined. Every molecule of CFCs 11 and 12 is more than 10,000 times as effective in warming up the earth than one molecule of carbon dioxide. Other industrial gases that destroy the ozone layer include nitrous oxides (which are released by nitrogenous fertilizers and by burning coal and oil). They are long-lived and can destroy the ozone. Methyl-chloroform is also destructive, but relatively short-lived.

Air conservation
What can we do to avoid polluting the atmosphere?
- Burn less fossil fuels, e.g. coal, and use solar energy. (Nuclear energy is an alternative, but also presents another set of problems.)
- Stop carbon dioxide being released into the atmosphere.
- Plant more trees to convert carbon dioxide in the air into oxygen.
- Gradually phase out the use of CFCs.
- Reduce the levels of chlorine in the stratosphere.

PLANTS

Plants provide food either directly or indirectly to both humans and animals. They also provide habitat, produce oxygen, modify climate, provide industrial raw materials for the production of rubber, paper and fibre, provide the raw materials from which most medicines are made, control soil erosion, conserve water, and provide fuel and timber for building. Humans have relied on plants for their livelihood and comfort since the beginning of time.

Over-exploitation

The present expansion of human population and advances in technology, have over-exploited the plant resources that are available. The over-exploitation has destroyed or partly depleted the land areas in which the plants live. In this way plant communities themselves have decreased.

Some of the destructive activities which have led to the decrease in plant communities include:

- **Clearing or burning** of large areas of vegetation for human settlement, farming, pasture, etc;
- **Uncontrolled destruction of forests** to satisfy the demand for timber, fuel, paper and furniture;
- **Overgrazing** of land due to overstocking of livestock;
- **The release of toxic gases** from industry into the atmosphere which either poisons vegetation directly or causes acid rain. These gases also cause a rise in the atmospheric temperature which reduces condensation in the clouds. This, in turn, decreases rainfall;
- **Over-use of agro-chemicals** on farms. The remains of these chemicals are washed into water bodies where they kill flora and fauna;

We must strictly control the current rate of human population growth in the world, if our efforts to conserve vegetation are to succeed.

Conservation of plants

We need to be aware that a problem exists with our environment. We all need a desire to change and we can start by looking at our own home, *shamba*, neighbourhood and country. Here are some of the things we can do:

- **Maintain tree cover** on mountains and hillsides to preserve water catchment areas. As long as tree cover is undisturbed, water supplies to the streams are regular. When the trees are destroyed, rivers and streams no

18

longer flow regularly. Where trees have been cut down, indigenous trees (those native to Kenya) should be planted. These trees will create once more the benefits of tree covered areas.

• **Use wood and paper** carefully in order to conserve trees. Paper is made from wood, so if you save paper, you preserve trees. The same with fuel wood.

•**Make compost** for the garden from kitchen and table waste. This will improve the soil both in texture and in water retention. Natural organic fertilizer, such as compost and animal manure is non-polluting, cheaper and much safer than chemical fertilizers which are expensive and can have nasty side effects on the environment.

° **Prevent pollution** by using biological control methods to kill pests in the shamba. By this we mean using natural predators, which prey on the pests. Destructive insects can also be controlled by sprays made from common plants, for instance stinging nettles. First soak them in water for 2 - 3 weeks. When the plants have broken down, strain the water through a sieve and use as a spray against insect pests. It is very effective and costs nothing. Another method is to crush 2 - 3 cloves of garlic, soak them in half a litre of water for 24 hours then dilute with 2 litres of water and use as a spray.

If you plant marigolds in between crops, you can keep pests away. If you leave areas of the *shamba* uncultivated, you can encourage birds and lizards to live there which will feed on pests and pollinate the crops. Bees will also help to pollinate crops.

• **Organize groups** among your friends and neighbours to:
    * Take advantage of conservation tours and lectures;
    * Gather seeds for tree planting;
    * Establish tree nurseries;
    * Hold tree planting campaigns to show how to care for seedlings;
    * Write to and visit local authorities to protest against forest clearing and industrial waste pollution;
    * Join conservation organizations such as the Wildlife Clubs of Kenya. These clubs are very active and organize outings, seminars and many other activities aimed at increasing awareness of the value of wildlife;
    * Support the National Parks and Reserves by visiting them. This will show the Government that Kenyans wish to conserve the wildlife and the beauty of these areas for their own enjoyment.

CHAPTER 3

The Significance of Wildlife and its Role in the Ecosystem

Wildlife conservation is the science of protecting and managing wildlife populations and their habitats for specific human objectives. To a conservationist, the word "wildlife" includes a wide range of all undomesticated creatures including mammals, reptiles, amphibians, birds, insects, fish, soil organisms and plants. Management may involve translocation (removing or transferring wildlife from one point to another), to reduce or increase their numbers. Alternatively, the wildlife species may be totally protected in their native environment and left untouched for nature to take its course.

The food chain

The very existence of humanity depends on the biological and ecological role played by all species of wildlife. These animals and plants range from micro-(very small) and macro-(very large) organisms in the soil to the giant land mammals and trees. All of them are basically inter-related and cannot be separated from one another. Within the ecosystem, each animals plays a part which compliments another. Together they form what is known as the food chain; for example:

- Soil supports all living things.
- Plants capture solar energy from the sun, and using carbon dioxide from the air, and water and minerals from the soil, manufacture their own food.
- Plant-eating animals (herbivores) get their food from plants which is changed into food energy in their bodies.
- Flesh-eating animals (carnivores) get their food energy from the flesh and blood of herbivores.

- When both herbivores and carnivores die, their bodies decompose (break down) and the nutrients (nitrogen, phosphorous, carbon, etc) from their bodies go back into the soil.
- These nutrients, which are essential for plant growth, are taken up by the growing plants, thus completing the nutrients cycle in the ecosystem.

Soil organisms

According to the <u>Encyclopaedia Britannica</u> (Vol. 16) about one thousand million organisms live in every one square metre of the rich topsoil. These organisms range from the microscopic single-cell bacteria to small mammals.

Micro-organisms include actomycetes, fungi, bacteria, algae, ciliate, protozoa and tardigrade.

Macro-organisms include mite, springtail, nematodes, fly-maggot, pauropod, slugs, proturan and potworms.

Megafauna are the largest soil organisms and include earthworms, moles, mice, snakes, lizards, insects, hares and rabbits.

Most of the soil organisms live at the litter layer (leaf-fall on the surface) and at upper stratum (the top two or three inches of soil depth). They move up and down the soil depth daily or seasonally depending on the temperature and moisture of the upper soil. Some organisms penetrate deep into the sub-soil through cracks and fissures (deep cracks).

Functions of soil organisms

Micro-organisms begin the decaying process as soon as plants and animals die. These organisms release carbon dioxide, nitrogen, sulphur and complex molecules like protein and acids into the soil for the future growth of young plants. Micro-organisms break down nitrogen compounds in soil and humus into simple compounds like nitrites and nitrates which can be used by growing plants. Green plants convert carbon dioxide from the air and water from the soil into organic plant substances. Animals eat these plants and convert their compounds into animal tissue.

Both **macro and mega-organisms** benefit the soil in several ways. Firstly they aerate (put air into) and drain the soil when they dig their tunnels. As they move through the compacted (hard packed) soil, they break it open and improve its aeration. Secondly, when soil animals (such as millipedes, woodlice and earthworms) eat the organic matter from animals and plants, it passes through their intestines and breaks down. This process releases mineral soil particles into the soil. Soil animals also help in the formation of soil nitrogen. This is because their faeces contain nitrogen in the form of ammonia, urea, uric acid and other substances which are used by plants.

Since most functions of micro and macro-organisms are beneficial, soils with large populations of these organisms are usually fertile and productive. We must therefore preserve soil organisms in order to maintain fertile soil for the production of food for humans and animals.

Insects represent an important link in the food chain. Scientists have identified over a million species which fall into several categories: e.g.

- beetles (*Coleoptera*)
- butterflies and moths (*Lepidoptera*)
- ants, bees, wasps (*Hymenoptera*)
- true flies (*Diptera*)

Although some insects destroy crops and others are carriers of disease, they form an important link in the food chain in the following ways:

- Insects are an important source of food for birds, mammals and reptiles.
- Insects also assist bacteria, fungi and other organisms to decompose organic matter, such as dead plants and animals, and to produce soil nutrients. For example, the decay of carrion (the flesh of dead animals) by bacteria is speeded up by the maggots of flies. Moths and beetles break down hair, keratin and feathers.
- In many parts of the world people eat insects like grasshoppers, locusts, termites and weevil grubs as a source of protein.
- Most flowering plants depend on insects for pollination and propagation.
- Lastly, termites bring up clay particles rich in mineral salts from near the water-table. These particles improve the soil texture.

Reptiles: Many people do not realise the importance of reptiles in the ecosystem. They are an important food item for birds of prey, carnivorous mammals and even for humans. In this way they fill yet another link in the food chain.

Although venomous snakes do exist, the majority of snakes found in Kenya are harmless and of great ecological importance. They control the population of harmful pests like rats, and help to keep their numbers down. Harmless snakes should be left alone and allowed to play their important part in our environment. However, if a poisonous snake is causing a problem, inform the Kenya Wildlife Service. They will capture it and put it in a snake park.

A venomous snake found in Kenya

Mammals and birds play an enormous role in the ecosystem. They enrich the soil by breaking down trees, bushes, shrubs and grass which are then eaten by smaller organisms down the line. The dung of mammals and guano of birds fertilize the soil. When they die, their body tissues are broken down by bacteria and become food for plants. Mammals and birds help in the propagation and dispersal of plant seeds. They carry them away, either attached to their bodies or in their faeces (dung and guano). The seeds are taken far from the parent plants and left there to be germinated by rain. In this way mammals and birds help propagate regeneration of the very vegetation on which they depend.

The Significance of Wildlife in Kenya

As we have seen, wildlife plays a vital role in our survival on this planet, Earth. However wildlife is not only important in terms of the ecosystem. It is also one of the major attractions of tourists to Kenya. The tourist industry directly supports over 100,000 jobs. It also encourages a further 200,000 people who produce handicrafts which are mostly bought by the tourists. Indirectly it promotes agricultural development since tourists create a larger demand for food both here and overseas. In this way wildlife has become the single most important foreign-exchange earner in Kenya today. For that reason alone we have to support and care for this valuable resource.

Many people ask why we need to protect the remaining species of wild animals and birds from extinction. They wonder why there is so much concern for environmental conservation.

At the beginning of the twentieth century, most of our countryside was unspoilt and nature took care of itself. The population of Kenyan pastoral, hunting or agricultural communities was small. They lived on the available resources without destroying them. They used a small fraction of the available resources leaving the basic stock untouched. This practice ensured that animals and plants could renew themselves and reproduce at their own speed.

Maasai herdsman with his flocks

However, during the first two or three decades of this century, medical services and modern agricultural methods were introduced into the country. This meant the child mortality rate was reduced. Many children grew to adulthood and adults lived longer. Modern farming methods ensured adequate food supplies for the expanding human population. As a result, the Kenyan population began to grow rapidly. In 1948 the population was 4.8 million. By 1989 the figure had grown to an unbelievable 24 million. This huge jump in population has seriously overburdened all public services and natural resources, including wildlife.

Human settlement for farming, ranching or habitation has taken up much of the land where wildlife used to roam freely. Today's hunter no longer hunts for food alone, but also for commercial gain from the sale of game trophies. Traditional beliefs which used to protect the wildlife have been discarded. As a result, hunters have over-exploited and destroyed wildlife and brought many species to extinction.

24

Causes of wildlife destruction

Why have wild animals disappeared from many parts of Kenya? Why have many wild animals been destroyed? Let us look at the causes:

Poaching for commercial profit and trophies (e.g. rhino horn and elephant tusks) is the main reason for the rapid decline in the elephant and rhino populations. The elephant population decreased from 165,000 in 1973 to 18,000 in 1988 and the black rhino population from 20,000 in 1970 to 350 in 1986, the lowest number ever. By mid 1992 elephant numbers increased to 26,000 and black rhino to a minimum of 410. This increase is due to careful conservation and strict control of poaching.

Wildlife habitats have been destroyed by deforestation, bush fires, water pollution and air pollution.

Expanding human settlement has confined wild animals to smaller and smaller areas and destroyed many habitats. There is no longer enough room for the previous number of wild animals because of the expanding human population. Settlements have blocked migration routes and prevented animals from dispersing and reaching their natural breeding grounds. As a result wildlife has overused some areas where they are forced to remain.

Exotic species from other countries have been introduced into the existing ecosystems. The introduction of new species often brings more problems than it solves. If the introduced species survives well, it may badly affect the native species and in the end the whole ecosystem. For example:

• **Nile Perch** was introduced into Lake Victoria in the early 1960s. The fish prey upon smaller species of fish like the Tilapia. As a result, the variety of the native species of fish in the Lake has decreased.

• **Coyup** was introduced into Lake Naivasha and caused the destruction of the water-lilies.

• *Salvinia molesta* was introduced into Lake Naivasha and caused problems with fish breeding in the Lake.

Neighbouring countries have failed to observe and enforce international laws and conventions which govern and protect migratory animal species. As a result poachers have killed those species whenever they moved across international boundaries. While one country bans hunting, another will license the same. This situation is incompatible with good conservation.

25

The attitudes of some countries towards conservation have not changed. They still trade in the trophies of endangered species because they do not realise, or do not care about, the desperate situation of wildlife. Attitudes are changing, but sometimes more slowly than we would wish.

Governmental conservation efforts

The Government of Kenya fully recognised the magnitude of the problem. They determined to save the remaining herds of wildlife for the enjoyment of the present and the future generations. In order to protect wild animals from destruction and eventual extinction the Government has taken measures which include the following:

- **National parks, reserves and sanctuaries** have been established to protect wildlife species and allow the wild animals and plants to breed in safety.

- **Scientific management practices** are used to control animal populations for their protection. e.g. translocating animals, providing waterholes and salt licks, controlled burning to improve pastures, etc.

- **Conservation laws and regulations** are enforced to make sure that poaching or illegal handling and dealing in game trophies is stopped.

- **Education** of the general public will create better conservation awareness. If people understand what conservation is all about, they will support its practices.

- **National and international co-operation** has been gained to observe and enforce the existing laws and conventions which protect wildlife, especially the endangered species.

The Role of the Individual in Wildlife Conservation.

To ensure a healthy environment and promote economic development, Kenyans should follow these guidelines:

- **Practise** the conservation measures outlined above.

- **Stop** using chemicals which poison and kill organisms, and pollute the soil and the water bodies of the country. For example, in 1983, Kenyatta National Hospital treated two people a day, on average, for chemical poisoning. Such poisoning was due to the large amount of pesticides used to kill insects in many parts of the country. Instead, change to biological control measures which add fertility and moisture to the soil by using animal manure or organic compost which is cheaper, harmless to the soil, and very beneficial.

- **Be aware** of any threat to the environment created by manufacturing companies or sewage disposal works. Refuse to allow immoral people to pollute the environment. Such pollution will eventually injure your health.

- **Respect** and allow wildlife to live in harmony with you. Wild animals can be used as tourist attractions. Alternatively, landowners can get government approval to ranch or farm wild animals for considerable economic gains.

- **Report** to wildlife conservation authorities whenever wild animals threaten human life or domestic animals. The authorities can capture such animals and remove them from the area. However, you should never poison them as the poison will itself go back into the soil and may eventually injure the health of the person who applies it.

Improper pesticide spraying eventually harms human and animal life

CHAPTER 4

Common Wild Animal Communities and their Habitats

A habitat is the natural home of a living organism, and forms part of its surroundings or environment. **Ecology** is the study of the inter-relationship between animals or plants and their environment. This inter-relationship is the way living organisms adapt themselves behaviourally and physically to the influences of their non-living environment. In turn, the living organisms influence the physical conditions of their surroundings. In this way the living plant or animal and its non-living environment interact. When these interactions between the living (plants and animals) and their non-living surroundings become self-supporting in a given area, they form a unit called an **ecosystem.**

Communities

For survival and security, wild animals live in structured societies such as large herds, small family groups, pairs or individuals. Ecologists have been studying such social systems for many years. However, they are only just beginning to understand the complex inter-relationships between various animal social systems, their ecology, and the types of habitats they live in. Ecological studies have shown how flexible animal social systems are, and how habitats influence their way of living. In general, herbivores or plains game such as wildebeest or topi form large herds which live in open grasslands. While animals which live in forests and bushlands, such as bushbuck or dik dik, live singly or in small groups. This strategy helps them to survive since large herds in thick forests would find it very difficult to escape from predators. A single animal or a small group can escape more easily through the bush.

Herbivores

Wildebeest form the largest aggregations (groups) of plains game in East Africa at certain times of the year. Wildebeest are grazers which feed on

28

short grasses. They appear in large numbers on open short-grass plains where their pasture is readily available. Some wildebeest populations are migratory. For example those of the Serengeti-Mara region migrate along a 500 kilometre circular route each year. This is an adaptation to take advantage of the fresh pastures in the newly visited areas while pastures in the abandoned areas have time to regrow.

In other parts of East Africa there are sedentary wildebeest populations which remain settled in one area. They live in small herds or family groups made up of mothers, juveniles, sub-adults and the new born. The territorial males live singly. This is a common system of social organization in wildebeest; females and the young live together in breeding herds while most mature males form bachelor herds. The prime males live alone and guard their territories, which they mark with their urine and dung. These males have a better opportunity to mate with females within their territory. They usually stand alone in elevated positions such as on top of a termite mound, advertising their status (social position) as territory owners. When their physical powers weaken they are defeated in fights and replaced by stronger bachelor males.

Hartebeest (Kongoni) are also gregarious (living in large groups) herbivores which live in open grasslands. They live in herds of females and young males which wander over many different territories held by independent prime males. Young bulls form bachelor groups which live in less favourable parts of the range (grassland). Some Hartebeest populations are migratory while others are sedentary.

Topi are similar in appearance to the hartebeest but have a darker coat colour. They are also gregarious herbivores, but are not migratory. Their social organization varies with the ecological conditions and their territorial systems take various forms. Open plains are ideal for the survival of both topi and hartebeest since they rely on their sight to escape from their enemies.

The Topi has a darker coat colour

Impala prefer lightly bushed or wooded grasslands. Their herds may consist of a number of females and their young, with a dominant territorial male. He is the owner of the herd but sometimes allows a few subordinate males within the herd. Other males live in bachelor herds in less favourable habitat. The dominant male mates with the females in his territory. Non-territorial males have less chance of mating with the females because the herd owner guards his females jealously and prevents outsiders from approaching them. Whenever predators attack, impala usually jump over the bushes or undergrowth and leave the predators stranded.

Buffalo are both forest and bushland dwellers. They are very gregarious and may form large herds consisting of hundreds of individuals.

During the breeding season, buffalo herds contain animals of both sexes and of various age groups. At other times adult male herds or bachelor herds stay away from the breeding herd. Buffalo bulls are non-territorial. Buffalo depend on water for drinking and wallowing in muddy pools. They are therefore found in areas where water is available. Beware: they may charge at any time.

Buffalo are dangerous and unpredictable

Eland, on the other hand, are nomadic and less dependent on water. They have a very efficient system of conserving their body water, therefore they can go for long periods without drinking and can thus make use of extremely dry ranges away from water. Their social organisation varies from time to time: sometimes an adult will accompany groups of young animals, at other times there will be no adult in attendance.

Elephant are both browsers (feeding from trees) and grazers (feeding from the ground). They live in family herds led by the oldest and most experienced female called the 'matriarch'. The family group consists of her relatives, sisters, daughters and their offspring. Young males leave the natal group into which they were born when they reach puberty, to join bachelor herds. Mature males join the breeding herds only during the mating season. Several large herds may occasionally aggregate when migrating or looking for water.

Common or Burchell's Zebra are grazers which are usually migratory and non-territorial. During migration, family groups aggregate into very large herds of several hundreds or even thousands of animals. However, under normal circumstances, they live in family groups of a stallion (male) and his harem (group of breeding females) of about 5-6 females and their young. When the young females from the group are grown up they are taken away by other stallions to join or form their harem. Young males will eventually leave to join bachelor herds.

Giraffe are browsers which live in bush or lightly wooded areas. Their browsing habits shape the vegetation (especially the acacias) to form what is called a 'browse-line'. They stay in small family herds which may join up into large groups as they wander about. Old males may live singly or form male groups.

A Maasai Giraffe

Black Rhino males are normally solitary animals but a female will commonly be accompanied by her calf, or by a male during mating. The calf of a black rhino walks beside or behind its mother. Rhinos stay within their home range even during drought and do not leave unless translocated. Black Rhino are usually browsers (leaf eating) and have an upper lip which is pointed and prehensile (can be used to grip) thus enabling them to browse the twigs and leaves of many different shrubs.

White Rhino, on the other hand, are usually grazers; the wide mouth has been adapted specially for eating grass. In fact, the word "white" is a corruption of the Afrikaans word for wide. They are gregarious animals and may live in large groups of up to 30 individuals. They are larger and not so aggressive as the Black Rhino although prime males sometimes show territorial behaviour. The calf of a white rhino walks ahead of its mother.

Carnivores

Lion are the most dominant of the African predators. They can live in different habitats, ranging from sea level through semi-desert, savannah and mountain forest to the snowlines of Mt. Kenya or Mt. Kilimanjaro. However, lion are most commonly found in open savannah or lightly wooded or bushed grasslands. Lion are the most social of the African cats. They often live in family groups called prides or related females may live together with their young. They are territorial and a new male lion wishing to settle in an area must defeat the previous territory owner. Then the defeated lion will run away and leave his family to the more dominant new-comer. The new male takes over the territory and the harem.

Lion hunt all herbivores and may even kill young elephant and rhino. When hunting singly or as a team, they approach their prey stealthily and then make a final short rush. Hunting is mostly by night, early morning or evening, although under certain conditions they may also hunt by day. When they are too ill or old to kill for themselves they scavenge on animals killed by other predators.

Spotted Hyena are social and territorial; they live in groups dominated by females which are usually larger than males. People often believe that hyena are only scavengers, but spotted hyena can be efficient hunters too. However they will also scavenge if a kill or carcass is available. For example they have been known to drive a lion away from its kill, especially when they attack as a pack.

Cheetah are territorial. They hunt by day but employ a different hunting method from that of a lion. The cheetah will run down its prey, relying on its speed. It is the fastest animal in Africa, and has been recorded at speeds of up to 110 kph (70 mph). Cheetah prefer to live in open grassland where they can run without being obstructed by bush or forest.

Its body shape is adapted to its style of hunting: it has long thin legs, a long, slender body, small head and non-retractable claws (it cannot draw the claws back into the paws). However it is a nervous and timid animal and will give up its kill to other predators or scavengers. Because they hunt by day when visitors are allowed in the park, they sometimes give up their efforts if disturbed by tourists.

The cheetah is the fastest animal on earth

Leopard are solitary, territorial and live in rocky, bushed or forested areas. They hunt by stalking (quietly moving closer to) their prey among rocks or forests and finally pouncing on it. Therefore thick forests, bushes or rocky cliffs are suitable for their survival. The leopard's dark, yellowish spotted body camouflages well with the forest tree leaves. It is therefore able to survive close to heavily settled areas because of its secretive behaviour.

Leopards prey on almost every other creature but prefer medium-sized herbivores like impala, bushbuck and baboons. After feeding, the leopard drags the remaining portion of the kill high up into the branches of a tree to save it from scavengers.

Leopards rest in the shade of forest trees

Natural conservation of habitats

Scientific studies show that wild animals do not cause serious destruction to their habitats as domestic animals do. This is true whether they live in small or large herds unless they are confined to small areas. Ecologists who have studied both domestic and wild herbivores and their feeding habits have come up with the following reasons for this:

Evolution: Wild African herbivores have evolved over millions of years through alternating periods of plenty and drought. They have therefore adapted to these changes for their survival; they have developed a system of rotational grazing and migration in succession. In this way they give each area a chance to regenerate.

Unlike livestock, wild animals use the whole range of available grass and forage materials. Warthog, Grant's and Thomson's gazelles feed on very short, tender growing grasses. Zebra, buffalo and eland may feed on the taller, coarser parts of the grasses. Browsers like black rhino, impala and bushbuck feed on the shrubs or at the middle level of the bushes, while giraffe and gerenuk feed on the tender shoots further up the bushes or on the hanging branches of tall trees. So, as we can see, wild herbivores use different levels of the vegetation. In this way they avoid serious damage to their habitat.

33

Water sources often determine the season for migration. The herds stay by permanent sources during the dry season and spread out during the rainy season when surface water is more plentiful and widespread. The grasslands and bushes where the animals concentrate during the dry-season are then given time to grow back before the next grazing period.

Water dependency: Some wild herbivores are less dependent on water than domestic stock. Therefore they can travel further and use wider areas of dry land than cattle. For example, the gerenuk rarely needs to drink as it gains moisture from the fleshy leaves it eats. Many wild herbivores feed during the night when humidity in the air condenses as dew on the grass and leaves. By doing this, the animals take in quite a lot of water. On the other hand, cattle feed mainly during the day when pastures are scorched so they need to drink daily and can only use pastures within easy reach of water.

Predation (the killing of one animal by another) also limits the size of wild animal populations. Predators keep the herbivore population in balance with the available pasture. They remove the weakly or sickly individuals. In this way a healthy herbivore population free of genetic weaknesses or diseases survives.

There is an interaction between predator and prey species: when the prey becomes scarce, the predator population declines which gives the prey species time to recover. When the prey becomes plentiful again, the predator population increases, and the cycle begins again. This results in the periodic ups and downs of the population of both species.

However, the larger mature animals, elephant, rhino and hippo, have practically no enemies, except humans. Their populations depend on climatic changes, floods, droughts and diseases to keep their numbers in balance with the food available. Poaching and hunting upset the delicate balance by removing the wrong group of animals, i.e. the healthy, large animals with good skins and horns or tusks instead of the small sickly ones.

Loss of habitats

Indigenous forests and bushlands have disappeared from many parts of Kenya. They have been cut down to make room for settlement or planting. As a result many wild animals which lived in bushland and forests have been exterminated from wide areas. The few herds that remain are now confined to small patches of forest and bushland. These areas include patches of forests in the countryside or the protected forest Reserves and National Parks on the slopes of Mt. Kenya, Aberdares and Mau ranges, Mt. Elgon, Arabuko Sokoke and the Kakamega forests.

The remaining bush and woodland wild animals are found in suitable habitats in the Rift Valley, Eastern and North-Eastern Provinces and at the Coast. The plains game (zebra, gazelle, hartebeest, topi and wildebeest) are mostly confined to the remaining grasslands in some parts of Eastern and North-Eastern Provinces and the Rift Valley, since the vast grasslands of the Rift Valley are now used for wheat farming.

However, it is an astounding fact that approximately 80% of Kenya's wild animals live outside the protected areas of the National Parks and Reserves.

Loss of migration routes

Human settlement and farming have also blocked migration routes. Therefore animals cannot reach their traditional water sources and grazing grounds. They are gradually confined to smaller and smaller areas where they destroy their habitats thereby causing their populations to decline. Laikipia and Meru districts are good examples where animals have experienced this problem. Elephants used to migrate from the Aberdares Mountains to Mt Kenya and down to the savannah woodlands of Samburu, Isiolo and to the present day Meru National Park area. Since their routes have been blocked, the animals have become disorientated (confused) because they cannot follow their traditional routes. Some of them have forced their way through heavily settled areas, and caused damage to both human life, farm crops and the wild animal populations themselves.

Wildebeest and zebra rest after their migration.

CHAPTER 5

Wildlife Conservation and Management

Wildlife Conservation and Management is *"the protection and manipulation of wild animal populations so as to keep them at optimal, diversified and harmonious levels with the environment in order to yield sustainable benefits to man."* (Kai Curry Lindahl)

The aims of such conservation and management of wildlife and wildlands is to provide opportunities for

- **Public recreation**
- **Preservation of plant and animal communities**
- **Scientific studies**
- **Protection of water-catchment and/or scenic areas.**
- **Economic gain.**

In Kenya wildlife is conserved in National Parks, National Reserves, Game Sanctuaries, Forest Reserves, Trustlands (communal lands under county councils) and in group or private ranches and farms.

National Parks
According to the International Convention for the Protection of Nature held in London in 1933, National Parks are areas:

Placed under public control, the boundaries of which cannot be altered or any portion be excised except by the competent legislative authority, i.e parliament.

Set aside for the protection of wild animals and wild vegetation, so that the authorities may propagate, protect and preserve them. They are also set aside to preserve objects of beauty, geological, pre-historic, historical, archaeological or other scientific interest. This is done for the benefit, advantage and enjoyment of the general public.

In which hunting is forbidden. It is also prohibited to kill or capture fauna, and to destroy or collect flora except by, or under the direction and control of, the park authorities.

Therefore, National Park authorities maintain areas as undisturbed as possible. No human population live in the areas, except for the staff that work there. No domestic animals use the areas for grazing or drinking water.

In Kenya the Minister responsible for Wildlife Conservation and Management establishes or declares the National Parks. This is done after consultation with the local authorities (county councils). When an area is declared a national park it is no longer a trustland but a stateland. The National Parks are established and managed by the Central Government or by a Board of Trustees appointed by the Central Government.

Game Reserves or National Reserves
These are areas where wildlife is protected and has precedence. However, some human habitation may be allowed and livestock may share the area with the wild animals. Usually, individuals, state governments or local authorities take the initiative to set aside the areas and manage them. After passing council resolutions to declare such areas as conservation units the Minister responsible for Wildlife Conservation and Management is then advised to gazette them as national reserves. The land remains a trustland (under the local authorities). Although the original human inhabitants may remain in the reserves, new immigrants are usually restricted or prohibited. The number of livestock is often limited. If the need for total conservation is great, the authorities may give more complete protection to some national reserves, or parts of them, by prohibiting human settlement and livestock altogether.

Wilderness Areas
These are wildlands where development of any kind is forbidden. Even road construction is prohibited and people can reach them only by foot or animal transport. Buildings and other facilities do not exist and visitors must take with them all their necessities such as food, water and shelter. There are no wilderness areas in Kenya.

Game Sanctuaries or Conservation Areas
These are usually established to give special protection to a specific plant or animal community which is either threatened with extinction or one only found in one particular area.

Land owners can also establish or declare such areas. They may do this if they want to protect a certain plant or animal community on their land. At the same time they may use the rest of the land for other purposes. Examples are the rhino sanctuaries on private ranches in the Laikipia District.

Black rhino have a prehensile upper lip

Wildlife, Conservation and Management Act

The sections, by-laws and regulations of the Wildlife Conservation and Management Act (Cap. 376 Laws of Kenya) give powers to the law enforcement personnel of KWS. They are empowered to physically protect the conservation areas against trespassers, poachers, honey collectors, fuel wood cutters, livestock grazing, and other destructive activities. They may construct game barriers such as moats and ordinary or electrified wire fences. This may give more effective protection to a specific area, or it may stop wild animals straying out of the conservation area into human settlements.

Regulations are made to prevent the dumping of industrial wastes into the conservation areas. They also prohibit aircraft flying so low that they disturb animals in the parks and reserves. The law enforcement personnel may arrest and prosecute any person who breaks the provisions of the Wildlife Conservation and Management Act or any of the by-laws or regulations made under the Act.

Physical Development Structures

The Park authorities build new or improve existing physical infrastructures in order to make full use of the national park and reserve areas as places of recreation and enjoyment. Such physical structures include:

> **Roads, bridges and airstrips** are constructed to give easy access to the Parks and Reserves. They enable tourists to enjoy the best game viewing, patrol operators to work more efficiently, and scientists to study various aspects of the park. Roads also create firebreaks and encourage drivers to stay on the official motorways. Uncontrolled

driving off the road destroys vegetation and exposes the range to soil erosion. Off-road driving occurs when the land is flat or on open plains, for example in Amboseli, Maasai Mara, Samburu and Nairobi.

Buildings are constructed for staff housing, offices, park gates, research stations and control posts. In all cases the authorities try to use natural materials (stone, wood, thatch, etc.) so that they can blend naturally into their surroundings.

Tourist facilities are built in the parks: these include lodges, hotels, hostels and campsites, game observation points and picnic sites, as well as service buildings (lodge or hotel staff housing, laundry, petrol station, waste disposal, etc). They often resemble a small village. When the lodges become too many, the view can destroy the natural beauty of the park. The authorities must therefore keep a balance between earning more revenue and visitor enjoyment. Many lodges may bring greater revenue but decrease the enjoyment for the visitors because of over-crowding. For example, Maasai Mara National Reserve is a beautiful reserve which was recently faced with a problem of over-development. Overcrowding on the Reserve roads caused stress to both tourist and wild animal alike. However the authorities have now identified the problem and will not permit more lodges or campsites in the Reserve. The current management policy is to spread out tourist pressures to the surrounding ranches.

Education facilities: museums, exhibits and interpretation centres have been set up in many parks. These explain the park's ecology and the behaviour of the various animals to be found there. Self-guided walks have been established in certain areas where visitors can follow sign-posts placed along the trails giving relevant information. Labels mark important trees, bushes and flowers. Leaflets offer additional information.

In Nairobi National Park, an active education centre provides various exhibits and an auditorium. Here groups can enjoy wildlife conservation lectures and filmshows. Such centres help visitors to appreciate what the parks have to offer and to understand management practices. Next to the Nairobi Park is the Animal Orphanage where visitors can observe wild animals more closely.

They are able to watch Rangers care for the animals and learn about their individual needs.

The aims of the education programmes are:

- to make Kenyans understand and appreciate the value of their wildlife and the various ecosystems in the country. This will generate concern and support for conservation;

- to generate revenue to support our conservation and management programmes;

- to offer all visitors to Kenya high quality recreational facilities for them to enjoy.

Many school children visit the Education Centre at Nairobi National Park

Research

Similarly, management practices are carried out after scientific research has indicated what specific conditions and problems exist in a particular area. Research covers the following concerns:

Collection of data on rainfall and soil conditions.

Monitoring the changes in vegetation and animal populations. This is done by measuring vegetation density and carrying out animal censuses (counting).

Assessment of plant and animal populations to find out whether any species is threatened or endangered.

Socio-economic studies to identify human and wildlife conflicts.

Animal behaviour and ecology.

Management practices

The information acquired through research helps the park authorities to decide and make suitable policies, management plans and work programmes. Some of the management practices which are carried out in the conservation areas are listed below.

Fencing: This may become necessary to confine animals within the protected areas and to prevent human intruders or domestic animals from entering the conservation areas. Ordinary or electric wire fences have been constructed along sections of the boundaries of Aberdares, Nairobi, Mt. Elgon and Meru National Parks and totally surround Lake Nakuru National Park. The partial fencing in Nairobi National Park prevents animals from straying onto city roads where they cause havoc to both animals and traffic.

If a park is completely fenced, it will be safe from outside destructive human activities and domestic animals. However migratory species will not be able to move out and will be confined within the park, accelerating destruction of their habitat. Such confinement cause inbreeding which may result in serious genetic depression (increased cases of deformity and disease). When such situations arise, it becomes necessary to manage animal populations and their habitats actively.

Animal Censuses: Counting the number of animals in the park gives the park manager information on the number of animal species in his area as well as the sex ratio and age groups in the herds. It also shows the animal dispersal pattern at any particular time of year, and the migration patterns.
In wildlife census, two methods are commonly used:

Total Count: This involves a survey of a given conservation area. All animals seen within the area are counted. The final count is based on the actual number of animals seen and counted.

Sample Count: A representative area of a known conservation region is selected. All the animals in it are counted. The final count is then based on an estimate using the information collected from the smaller area. This is arrived at by using the following formula where the population for the whole area is the number of animals flushed, divided by the area of strip and multiplied by the total area.

$$P = \frac{A Z}{2 Y X}$$

where

P = population
A = Total area of study
Z = Number flushed
Y = Average flushing distance
X = Length of strip.

(Wildlife Management Techniques Manual; S.Schemnitz)

In both total and sample counts either aerial (using a light aircraft) or ground (on foot or in vehicles) techniques of counting may be used.

In conservation areas, wildlife managers carry out censuses of some important species. They are either important for economic reasons, cause changes in habitat, are migratory or threatened species. The most commonly counted species are elephant, rhino, zebra, buffalo, wildebeest, lion, cheetah, leopard and hyena.   The frequency of census depends on several conditions: whether transport and personnel are available; management policies; and the need to update records of any changes to animal populations .

High concentration of animals around water holes causes soil erosion

Water Supplies: In areas where there are no permanent sources of water, the park authorities may construct dams to hold water during the dry seasons. They may also provide piped water. In all cases, the water supplies in the parks should be evenly distributed. If the watering points are not spread throughout the park, the concentration of animals around watering points causes soil erosion. Artificial water supplies also help to keep animals within the park boundaries during the dry season. Without water supplies many of the animals might move out of the park to look for water. Artificial water points are provided in Nairobi, Tsavo and Nakuru National Parks.

Burning: Pastoral groups have practised the burning of vegetation in Africa since ancient times in order to improve grazing land. Burning removes long, matted, dry grass which has low nutritional value. It encourages fresh, succulent growth. In parks and reserves park managers can use burning to control the distribution of animals. In this way they reduce over-grazing in certain areas. The fresh grass after burning will attract animals to recently burned areas. Meanwhile the unburned areas are left to regenerate. However, burning can have a long term destructive effect in areas of low rainfall where the vegetation recovery rate is low. This is because burning removes the vegetation cover and leaves the soil exposed to erosion for a long time before the new plant cover grows. Good management will ensure that burning is done in rotation to avoid this problem.

Burning is often carried out immediately after the rains have started. This is to avoid burning tinder dry vegetation which burns very fiercely, creating hot fires. These hot fires destroy both plant root systems and the invertebrates living in the soil.

Salt Licks: Herbivores need salt and other minerals. They usually get them from salt and mineral licks which occur naturally. Carnivores get all the minerals they need from the flesh and blood of their prey. However artificial salt licks help keep herbivores within park boundaries because they provide what the animals need close at hand. This also ensures that the animals are available for the visitors to view. Salt licks may be seen at the Ark and Treetops Lodges in Aberdares National Park and at Voi Safari Lodge, Ngulia Lodge and Salt Lick Lodge in Tsavo West National Park.

Control of Predators: If the number of predators in a conservation area is considered too high for the herbivore population, then the park management may trap and translocate a number of the predators. They will be taken to other areas with higher herbivore populations. For instance, in 1990 three lions were translocated to Lake Nakuru National Park to keep the waterbuck population down.

Cropping and Culling: Sometimes the population of a particular animal species grows to such a size that it threatens the rest of the ecosystem. Then the park management may decide to reduce the over population by selective killing of a certain class of the animals such as the males, females, young, immature or old individuals. This is known as culling and it is done in one operation. Afterwards the carcasses may or may not be used. On the other hand, the practice known as cropping is done over a sustained period. The operation removes extra numbers from the over populated herds and the resulting products from the carcasses, such as hides, meat, horns, ivory and bones are used.

" I just know that elephant's around here somewhere."

Game ranching and farming
Game ranching and farming are good ways of managing wild animal populations to generate economic returns.

44

Game ranching: This is when ranchers keep or allow wild animals, especially herbivores, on their ranch to live separately or along with their livestock. From time to time, the ranchers carry out a census to find out the rates of the animals breeding, reproduction and mortality (death). From these findings, the rancher is able to decide how many of each species can be harvested monthly or yearly. The animals are killed and the meat sold locally or exported. The ranchers may use the other products in various ways. Examples of this kind of farming are Galana Game Ranch at the coast and the Athi River Hopcraft Ranch at Kapiti Plains.

Game farming: Farmers keep tamed or half-tamed wild animals under intensive farming conditions, breeding the animals and rear the young under intensive veterinary care until they are mature enough to be slaughtered. The meat is sold locally or exported.

Examples of game farming are the crocodile farm at Bamburi near Mombasa and the ostrich farm at Oltepesi in Kajiado District. The meat, eggs, feathers and skins from these farms are sold locally and exported. This practice ensures that the animal species survives while at the same time earning the country foreign exchange.

The male ostrich has black and white feathers

Park regulations

Park regulations help the park authorities to protect their conservation areas from bad practices and misconduct by visitors when in the parks. At the same time they help to maintain the security and enjoyment of the visitors. They are not meant to inconvenience the visitors but to help them have a pleasant visit. Visitors are therefore requested to observe these regulations for their own interests.

> **Transport:** If you visit a park make sure that your vehicle is both in good condition and protects your passengers properly. Park authorities will

not normally allow pick-ups or open trucks into the parks/reserves. They will also deny entry to vehicles with noisy exhaust systems.

Visiting Times: Visitors are not allowed to be in the park at night or during the hours of darkness between 7 pm and 6 am. Entry is forbidden after 6.15 pm.

Entry: Always enter and leave the park through official entry gates and pay the required fee.

Weapons: It is an offence to be in possession of weapons, ammunition, poison, explosives or traps into a national park.

Business: It is also an offence to put up any form of advertisement or carry out any form of business in the park unless authorised by the Director of KWS.

Fires: Do not light fires or throw cigarette ends out of car windows. Fires can start very easily. They may quickly get out of control and can engulf the whole park. Fire endangers the lives of both you and the wildlife. If you see fire in the park, report to the park authorities immediately.

Pets: You are not allowed to take pets into parks or reserves. They may frighten wild animals or cause a stampede (running about madly). They may also provoke the animals which may react aggressively and affect the safety of visitors. They can also transmit diseases to their wild cousins.

"Now Fifi, behave yourself. Don't scare the poor beasties!"

Speed: The speed limit in the park is 40 km per hour. This is because animals may trot or jump across the road when you do not expect it.

Noise: You will disturb the animals if you make a noise or hoot while inside the park. Making noise will also annoy other visitors and may spoil your chance of good viewing.

Alighting from Vehicles: You may only get out of your car at a designated campsite, picnic site, self-guided nature trail or game observation point. Animals are friendly to passing vehicles but may attack if they see a human being on foot.

Short Cuts: It is an offence to drive off the park roads to get closer to animals or get a better view. Off-road driving does a lot of damage: it destroys the beauty of the landscape and the vegetation; it exposes the land to soil erosion; it also disturbs the animals and upsets their breeding and feeding habits. In addition you may get stuck in holes or mud if you leave the road.

Fishing: Fishing is not allowed in national parks/reserves. However, traditional or sportfishing may be allowed in the marine national reserves under licence. If you are in doubt, consult the local fisheries officer or the local park warden.

"So now what do we do?"

Wildlife: Animals have the right of way. Stay at a safe and respectful distance, especially when watching buffalo, elephant or rhino. Their behaviour is quite unpredictable; they may not want to be disturbed. Do not entice, touch or feed wild animals. If you feed them, you may affect their health badly. Alternatively, they may attack you or other visitors in search of food once they get used to being fed.

Hiking: Hiking or horse riding is not allowed except in Hells Gate National Park and the mountain national parks where moorland walking is permitted . This is usually at high altitudes after the visitor has driven to the highest possible limits.

Swimming in Rivers or Lakes: Crocodiles live in most Kenyan rivers and fresh water lakes. Visitors are therefore warned not to swim in the rivers or lakes. Drawing water must be done with great care as crocodiles may snap at the slightest opportunity.

Natural Objects: Do not remove rocks, fossils, skulls, horns, shells, corals, plants, wild flowers, nests and all other natural, pre-historical, historical or archaeological objects from the park. They should be left as you found them in their natural setting so that other people may discover and enjoy them. Do not write, paint or carve your name or slogan on tree trunks, rocks or on cave walls as this damages the beauty of the park and is prohibited.

Camping: Camping is allowed only in the designated campsites. You must first get a permit from the Director or the Warden in charge of the park or reserve.

Camp Fires: These are allowed only at designated campsites. Light them away from bushes or grasses. Keep fires small and under control at all times. When you leave the campsite, pour water on the camp fire and cover the place with soil or sand. Never leave smoking or smouldering firewood behind.

Litter: Litter is ugly and can be dangerous. Broken glass or shiny tin can magnify the sun's rays enough to start a fire. If animals feed on litter, their health and lives are in danger. In 1990 for example, garbage poisoned an elephant in Amboseli National Park. Its stomach contained clothing, polythene, paper and bottle tops. In campsites, visitors must hide waste carefully in dustbins or burn it. They must take away empty containers such as cans, bottles, foil packs, etc and get rid of them outside the park. Animals such as baboons, monkeys and hyena like to scavenge on human food and garbage. When they become accustomed to human food, they attack vehicles and rob campsites in search for more.

Rubbish is unsightly and a danger to birds and animals.

Human Waste: If there are no lavatories or latrines, dig a hole or trench away from campsites, picnic sites, game observation points, nature trails or water sources. Cover the human waste completely with soil or rocks.

Snakes: If you see a snake in the park, remember, it requires nothing from you but the chance to get out of your way. It is always safer to leave it alone.

REMEMBER:

When in the Park......
Leave nothing behind but your footprints,
Take nothing but photographs!
Let it not be said after you
That all was well.....
Before you came.

CHAPTER 6

Wildlife Conservation in Conflict with Human Interests

As you have read in previous chapters, wild animals have lived together with humans on this earth since time immemorial. Except in isolated cases of self-defence or when a wounded, sickly or aged predator turns to man-eating as the last resort for survival, normal wild animals do not deliberately attack and kill human beings. They have learned over the years to fear humans. Similarly, the big herbivores (elephant, rhino, hippo and buffalo) will normally only attack humans in self-defence or in defence of their young.

Today, other conflicts occur when wild animals, especially carnivores, attack and kill domestic animals. This occurs when the predators' legitimate prey animals are not available because of poaching and human encroachment, and so domestic stock become the easiest targets. A sick or wounded predator which is not strong enough to hunt down a wild animal may attack domestic stock for the same reason. Herbivores may sometimes invade cultivated fields and crops, causing destruction to plants and fences and transmitting diseases to livestock. Let's look more closely at these conflicts between wild animals and humans:

Wild animals that threaten human life
These can be divided into two categories:

Predators: Lion, leopard, hyena and sometimes wild dog and crocodile come into this category. Although pythons have been known to attack and kill people, such cases are rare. If a mammalian predator is wounded, ill or very old, it may become a man-eater as the only way to survive. This is because they become too weak to hunt down and kill their usual prey. In other cases predators may attack humans because their legitimate prey species has become scarce or when reacting in self-defence.

- Fortunately, the mobility of crocodile is limited to lakes, rivers and river banks. To avoid crocodile attacks do not swim, bath or even draw water from crocodile infested rivers or lakes.

• Pythons lie quietly in tall grass or thick bushes where they ambush and grab unsuspecting prey. They bite and quickly coil themselves around the prey. Pythons constrict the prey (tighten their coils around it until it dies) and then swallow it whole.

• Kenya Wildlife Service personnel can capture crocodiles, pythons and other dangerous venomous (poisonous) snakes and translocate them to special areas for tourist viewing or to the Snake Park at the Headquarters of the National Museums of Kenya in Nairobi.

Animals that kill humans in self-defence. All wild animals fear human beings and usually avoid them. The larger mammals like elephant, rhino and hippo have almost no enemies except humans who have hunted them for meat and trophies for centuries.

• **Elephant** and rhino have poor eye-sight. They rely on their senses of smell and hearing to warn them of the presence of humans. They will trumpet and snort to scare away an enemy. They only attack as a last resort or in an attempt to escape, especially when they did not sense the presence of humans in time to run away. If left unharmed they will normally run away.

• **Hippos** will attack and kill a human in water when disturbed. On dry land they will attack if the enemy comes between them and the water which is their escape cover. They will also attack a boat or water craft if it is too near and seen as a threat to their herd or young.

• **Buffalo** have good eye-sight and will normally run into thick bush to escape. However, if they did not hear or sense the presence of a human until it was too late they will attack in order to get a chance to escape. However, like most wild animals, buffalo which are wounded, alone or with calves can be extremely aggressive and may attack without being molested or disturbed. Buffalo are generally very unpredictable and dangerous.

"We can't save him now, Pete. He's infested with crocodiles!"

Animals that kill livestock

Lion, hyena, leopard, cheetah, wild dog, crocodile and python are the main animals responsible for killing livestock in Kenya. To avoid this problem, farmers should guard their domestic animals during the day and put them behind strong fences or walled enclosures at night. When predators do kill livestock, the Kenya Wildlife Service should be contacted immediately. They will trap the offending animal and translocate it to an area away from human settlement.

Under no circumstances should untrained people try to follow the predator into the bush to kill it. Injury or death is often the result. The use of poisoned bait to kill the predator is forbidden because it is dangerous. It may affect the environment or cause the death of other innocent wild animals or people.

Wild animals which transmit diseases to humans and livestock.

Wild animals can transmit diseases such as rabies, foot and mouth disease, rinderpest east coast fever, malignant catarrh and trypanosomiasis. A diseased animal can pass on rabies to either a human or beast in its bite. Wild animals such as buffalo can transmit foot and mouth disease to livestock. The wild animals themselves have immunity (natural protection) to the parasites and the disease. Ticks carry rinderpest and east coast fever. They may infect cattle after biting the wild herbivores.

A blood parasite that causes trypanosomiasis may live in wild herbivores without harming them. When transmitted by the tsetse fly to human beings it can cause sleeping sickness. In cattle it will cause a disease known as *nagana* .

Malignant catarrh is a viral disease carried by wildebeest in their placentas (birth sacks). When the mother gives birth, she drops the placenta onto the grass together with the virus. When cattle feed on the grass they swallow the virus. It enters their blood stream and attacks the mucus membrane on the inside of the nose and throat, killing the animals.

To avoid these dangers, farmers should keep their livestock and wild animals separate as much as possible. They should also dip their livestock regularly. If livestock do catch a disease, farmers should report to the nearest veterinary officer as soon as possible. Alternatively, they should seek help from the Veterinary Department Headquarters in Muguga or from Kabete Wildlife Disease Section.

Wild Animals which destroy crops

Occasionally wild herbivores and wild pigs may invade cultivated land and destroy crops. This often causes serious damage. Monkeys, baboons, porcupines and birds such as quelea, guineafowl and spurfowl also destroy crops.

The Laikipia Plains and Meru District suffer most from elephant damage. This is because large scale ranching and farming in the districts have blocked the traditional migratory routes from Aberdare Mountains to Mt Kenya and down to Meru National Park. Therefore the animals, especially elephants, are denied their traditional grazing areas and cannot reach their breeding grounds.

Elephants denied their migratory
routes may destroy crops

Electric fences have proved effective in preventing wildlife damage to crops. These fences give the animals an electric shock when they try to go through. If there are no electricity supplies to the area, then solar energy is used.

53

Where elephant are not a problem, barbed or chain-link wire fences are sufficient. Ditches or moats (ditches filled with water) are useful, if they are dug properly and maintained to make them game-proof. They will stop animals from crossing into settled and farmed areas. Where livestock rearing is not involved, farmers are advised to encourage leopards in the surrounding bush or forests. Such carnivores help to control the populations of bushpig, monkeys and baboons.

Wild animals endangered by human interests

Wildlife conservation is faced with a number of problems which threaten the survival of wildlife both within and outside the conservation areas. Human beings have caused most of the problems which are identified below.

Poaching

Poaching is the illegal killing (except in self-defence) or capture of wild animals and marine life. It can be classified as subsistence and commercial poaching.

Subsistence poaching is when people kill wild animals illegally as a traditional source of meat. When the human population was small, subsistence poaching was harmless. It helped to keep the wild animal populations in balance with the available pasture. Because the present human population has increased enormously, subsistence poaching would destroy the remaining wild animals. It therefore cannot be allowed.

Commercial poaching is when people kill wild animals illegally for their trophies. It is more dangerous than subsistence poaching because the poachers kill every available mature and healthy animal, including potential mothers, in order to satisfy the demands of the game trophy markets. Commercial poaching has caused our wild animal populations to decline rapidly. As a result many wild animal species have disappeared from parts of Africa. For example, in Kenya the elephant population declined rapidly from about 165,000 to 18,000 and rhino from 20,000 to 350 between 1968 and 1988. Elephant and rhino are some of the most endangered species in Kenya, and indeed, the whole of Africa. Poachers kill elephants for their ivory which they sell to well organised business people. These traders pay the poachers a small amount of money while making huge profits for themselves by selling the ivory.

Poachers kill rhino for its horn. Rhino horn is in great demand in Asia because the people there believe it has medicinal qualities. The horn is ground into powder, mixed with water, and drunk. People used to believe that it was an aphrodisiac (stimulates the sexual appetite). Today, however, we know that it can only lower fever. In Yemen, they carve rhino horns and use them as expensive handles for daggers and knives.

In the 1960-70's poachers hunted the spotted cats, leopard and cheetah. Their skins were sold and made into very expensive coats, bags and jackets.

"I'm going to find that elephant if it's the last thing I do!"

In Kenya a ban on game trophy dealing in 1977 and 1978 almost stopped the trade. At almost the same time, world opinion turned against the mass killing of these beautiful and endangered creatures. Europe and North America have banned this trade in game trophies; in Arabia and the Far East some commercial trade in endangered game trophies still continues, most of it smuggled from Africa.

At local and international levels poaching can be stopped through enforcement of strict game conservation laws and regulations. Regional co-operation ensures that international conservation laws and conventions are enforced. Such laws govern and protect migratory animal species when they move across the international boundaries. Fortunately, due to the strong global campaign against commercialization of game trophies, the attitude of the international community towards this grisly trade has changed and the populations of endangered species are increasing annually.

More importantly, education will make local and international communities more aware of the desperate situation of the endangered wild animal species. Education will change the attitude of mankind towards the commercial trade in game trophies, even in those countries where the trade still exists. Hopefully, this will lead to the end of commercial poaching throughout the world.

Human encroachment

This occurs when expanding human populations move into and take away land set aside for the conservation of wildlife. The encroachment may be for settlement, cultivation or livestock ranching. This development has several bad effects on the future of wildlife:

Natural wildlife habitats are cut down and destroyed. This leaves the animals with no food, shelter or escape cover.

Wildlife populations lose their dispersal areas and are confined to smaller areas. The result is over-population and, in time, serious competition for food, breeding grounds and interference with breeding habits. Sadly, many wild animal species disappear.

These factors cause populations to decline and many species become extinct. For example, poaching is no longer a problem for the cheetah. However human settlement continues to destroy their habitat.

The wild dog population is also declining. The reasons for this are probably human encroachment and the destruction of their habitats. In addition they may be suffering from diseases transmitted from their domestic cousins and probably genetic depression. Research investigations are continuing to identify the causes of their population decline and to find ways of increasing their numbers.

A wild dog

Where poaching and disease are not the cause of decline, the destruction of habitat is usually to blame for species becoming endangered. For this reason, the authorities have established special reserves and sanctuaries to protect some of the rare species of plants and animals from further danger. Good examples of these are listed below.

- The Kakamega National Reserve was established to preserve the rare tropical rain forest species of mammals, reptiles, birds, butterflies and vegetation;

- The Tana River Primates National Reserve was created to protect the red colobus monkey and the crested mangabey;

- Saiwa Swamp National Park preserves the rare sitatunga antelope;

- Maralal Game Sanctuary protects various species of wild animals found near the town.

The solution to the human encroachment problem lies with the Kenyans themselves. They must understand that their population growth rate of 3.8% is one of the highest in the world. This enormous human population growth seriously strains the country's natural resources. It also reduces the quality of the various services (medical, education, food supplies, etc) which the Government wants to provide for its people. If we do not stop this growth rate, the exploding human population will demand more and more land for settlement. At present, the land is being taken away from the wildlife which is one of Kenya's greatest assets.

Pollution
Water, air and noise pollution sometimes threaten wildlife conservation areas as noted in Chapter 2. This occurs when effluents from urban sewage systems flow into the conservation areas and bring in pollutants. The pollutants kill aquatic fauna and flora. Lake Nakuru National Park is a good example of a conservation area which has severe pollution problems. Garbage, noise, vehicle traffic and fumes cause both visual and environmental pollution. If anti-pollution laws are enforced, this will help. However, Kenyans must learn to keep their environment clean.

Over-utilization
Too many tour companies with hoards of visitors cause many problems to our conservation areas.

Off-road driving is one such problem. It is caused by drivers who want to satisfy the visitors' desire for game viewing. The animals become scared and feel trapped by the vehicles. Also they cannot feed and mate naturally without their privacy. Eventually, this may force the animals out of the conservation areas.

Off-road driving also destroys the park vegetation. This destruction exposes areas to soil erosion.

"...And that ridiculous rule prohibiting open vehicles in the Parks.

CHAPTER 7

Modern Tourism in Kenya

The International Union of Official Travel Organization defines a tourist as:

"Any traveller who resides for a period of 24 hours or more in a country other than that in which he usually resides."

There are several different kinds of tourists: there are those tourists who come to Kenya from another country purely for pleasure and recreation; there are business people who, during the course of their stay, visit a tourist resort for recreation; and there are local travellers who visit other parts of the country for pleasure and recreation and who are called domestic tourists.

How did tourism start?

Before modern tourism developed, East Africa had very early contacts with ancient Greece, Arabia, Persia (now Iran) and India. Archaeological finds prove that these contacts stretched from Lamu to the shores of Lake Victoria and Lake Turkana. More recently, before 1890, visitors were usually adventurous explorers and missionaries. Many of these suffered at the hands of warlike tribesmen and slave traders. Commercial tourism as we know it today did not exist. However in 1929, the British Commercial Service linked East Africa by air with European cities. At this time, Europe become a possible source of tourists to the region.

After the defeat of the Germans in World War 1, Britain completely dominated over the East African region. This situation helped to create a close economic and political unity. The first Governors' conference in 1926 made several important decisions to support co-operation in the region. In 1948 the East African High Commission was established which further strengthened the co-operation. From 1948 onwards, the three East African territories, Kenya, Uganda and Tanganyika (as it was then known), shared many services. These services were essential for the development of tourism and included East African Railways and Harbours, East African Airways,

East African Posts and Telecommunications, Immigrations and Customs. In addition the British administration helped create uniform laws and regulations for the conservation and management of national parks and tourism.

At about the same time in Europe, industries were rapidly developing. Labour laws were developed to protect the rights and interests of the increased workforce. The International Labour Organization supported the right of workers to receive paid holidays. As a result, a wider section of the community had the freedom to travel where they wished. However the move towards world travel only started when three basic factors were fulfilled:

- Free time and paid holidays

- Increased income

- Better transport and the introduction of cheap charter flights and package tours.

Before Independence in 1963, Kenya had already built up a considerable foreign tourist trade and during the 1950s, 30,000 to 40,000 visitors a year came to Kenya. In the 1960s the situation changed dramatically when the numbers almost doubled from 61,352 to 117,000 by 1967. The number of tourists continued to grow throughout the 1970s by an average of 12% per year. In 1976 a total of 424,000 tourists were recorded and by 1991 this figure had grown to 804,000.

Accommodation
The amount of accommodation has also increased dramatically since Independence. In 1963, 5,840 beds were available and by 1988, 42,000 beds. The number is rising steadily all the time. Tourist hotels are well positioned and easily accessible to tourists. They have well-trained staff and are equipped with modern facilities such as bedrooms with their own bathrooms. The number of occupied bed nights rose from 2.2 million in 1971 to 5 million in 1986.

The following countries and regions provide the highest number of tourists to Kenya: Germany, United Kingdom, USA, Switzerland, Italy, France and Scandinavia.

Tourism Resources
The Arab and Portuguese traders left the Kenyan coastline with cultural, artistic and architectural monuments which are visual reminders of our history. Some archaeological sites have great significance worldwide, for

example Koobi Fora on the eastern shores of Lake Turkana.

However, the major tourist attraction is wildlife. This together with magnificent scenery, miles of beaches and a good climate make the country a tourist paradise. Kenya is particularly attractive because tourists can combine a beach holiday with excellent wildlife viewing.

In the past tourists have visited only a few game parks and the beach resorts, and have had no opportunity to observe Kenyan culture and traditions. This situation is changing; new tourism development strategies will ensure that in future tourists will travel more widely to the rural areas of the country. At present the Government is developing tourist infrastructures in areas where tourists have rarely gone. These include Western Kenya, the Rift Valley and North Eastern Province.

Wildlife and Tourism

Wildlife is the main resource of Kenyan tourism. The industry would lose its major attraction if it lost its wildlife. Foreigners come to see the herds of game, the annual migrations of wildebeest and zebra and the rare wild animals like bongo, white rhino, giant forest hog and the abundant bird and marine life. Fifty five national parks and reserves have been gazetted since 1946. These cover 7.7% of Kenya's land area, which shows the importance of Kenya's wildlife.

Types of tourism

Mass Tourism: This kind of tourism involves large numbers of travellers or tourists; an institution usually organises their journeys and they travel under the guidance of a tour guide or other qualified person. The institution also pays for their expenses and negotiates discounts or concessional low rates on the group booking.

Travel agents organise "package tours"and members of the tour make one payment. This payment includes charges for transport, airport taxes, accommodation, park entry fees, etc. These tours are cheaper for the tourists than if they were to travel individually. However "package tours" are not as profitable to the countries they are visiting because of the discounts involved.

Conference Tourism: In 1973, the Kenyatta International Conference Centre (KICC) opened in Nairobi. Since then, Nairobi has earned a good reputation as a conference centre, not only for Africa but for the world. A former USA Ambassador to the United Nations, Andrew Young, described the KICC as "The world's best designed Conference Centre" (April, 1985).

Facilities include: a conference room capable of seating 4,500-5,000 people; an amphitheatre seating 900 at tables on three tiers; a wide range of services such as banks, travel agents, telex, fax and international telephones to make communications between conference members and their home countries possible; and a fully equipped press gallery for journalists.

The Kenyatta International Conference Centre

Business Tourism: Nairobi has become an international city with regular flights to many industrial and commercial centres of the world. In addition, many international companies and large corporations have their offices in Nairobi. Since the business person is a good source of revenue for Kenya's tourism industry, various organisations have made efforts to develop business tourism in the country.

Sports Tourism: Since Independence, Kenya has become a great sporting nation. This is true not only in Africa but throughout the world. From time to time many sportsmen and women meet in Nairobi to take part in sporting events. They often come in large numbers. While they are in Kenya, many of them visit the national parks or reserves and relax on the beaches. Such visitors form another group of tourists.

Domestic Tourism: The Government of Kenya is following a policy to encourage tourism amongst the citizens and residents of Kenya. This has three purposes:

- It will help Kenyans to understand how important it is to maintain and preserve our wildlife and cultural heritage.

- It will help to keep the tourist industry busy and profitable at times when foreign tourists do not visit Kenya in such numbers. To achieve this, domestic tourists will receive low season and local resident rates. In this way thousands of jobs in tourism will be safeguarded.

- It will encourage ethnic integration and peaceful co-existence between Kenyans.

- It will encourage equal development in all areas of the country

The Socio-economic Value of Tourism

Tourism is Kenya's number one foreign exchange earner. Therefore its importance to the country's economy cannot be overemphasized. Foreign exchange earnings have increased from Ksh 160 million in 1963 to Ksh 11.9 billion in 1991. The industry requires few imports, produces a significant amount of revenue and requires no subsidies such as grants or loans from the Government.

The Central Government budget receives income from tourism. This income is collected from excise and customs duties, airport taxes, sales tax, accommodation tax, hotel training levy, entry fees to parks and reserves, concessional or rental fees paid by game lodges and camp-sites, company taxes and income taxes from individuals working in the industry.

Employment and Tourism

Tourism has greatly increased employment opportunities and earnings. Many people have the chance to become self-employed in tourist related services. In 1977 there were about 62,600 wage earners in trade, restaurants and hotels and by 1990 this number had grown to well over 100,000. In addition, more than 200,000 people depended on the industry indirectly.

Other socio-economic factors benefitted by tourism:

Standard of Living: The industry encourages social changes. Increased income among the people often causes these social changes. Tourism also encourages Government to improve communications (both transport and telephonic). It is often responsible for changes in fashion, diet, sports, etc.

Culture and Traditions: Through tourism local people have contact with different cultural and traditional values. These are reflected in music, dance, fashion, decoration, art, craft, sculptures, etc.

Mining: Tourists like to buy jewellery made with semi-precious stones. This demand has helped develop the mining of such minerals which would otherwise have remained unused in the soil.

Motivation to Work: Tourists have created an enormous demand for souvenirs and food. This need has motivated local people to undertake and develop tourist-orientated projects.

Industrial Development: Visitors from overseas help to create a demand for new goods. This demand encourages local manufacturers to produce new goods, and to achieve a higher standard of production. When they return home, visitors help to create a demand for our local agricultural and mineral raw materials.

Tourists enjoy a high standard of accommodation in Kenya.

Technological Development: Through tourism Kenya has increased its foreign exchange. This has meant that the Government can import a wider range of goods, such as televisions, videos, vehicles, cameras, for Kenyans to enjoy. In order to maintain and repair these imported goods the workforce has had to improve its own technical knowledge. This knowledge has enabled Kenyans to improve and increase production.

Agricultural Market: Tourism creates two important markets for our agricultural products: Firstly, farmers have to produce more food such as eggs, chickens, milk, meat, fruit and vegetables to provide thousands of tourists with top quality food; Secondly, the tourists who come to Kenya are impressed by our locally produced goods such as tea, coffee, fruit and flowers. They influence the business communities in their own countries to import Kenyan products. These exports again help to build foreign exchange for Kenya and create more employment.

Infrastructure: Tourists from overseas demand high standards not only of accommodation and catering but also transport and communications. To satisfy their needs, the Government is constantly making improvements to airports, harbours, highways, tele-communications, training centres, hotels and restaurants. These improvements also benefit the citizens and residents of Kenya.

Peace and Co-operation: Peace and stability in a country is essential for the tourist industry. African countries which recognise the benefits of tourism seek to maintain peace and co-operation both internally and abroad. Tourists will not visit countries which suffer from internal strikes and riots for fear of their own safety.

Problems Affecting Tourism

Regional and global events can badly affect tourism. Below are some events from recent history.

- Huge increases in oil prices from 1973 caused increased travel costs.
- Recession in world economies since 1973 reduced imports from African countries. Therefore foreign exchange decreased.
- Political unrest in Africa has limited the flow of tourists. For example, the closure of the Kenya/Tanzania border in 1977, sanctions (ban on trade) with South Africa, and troubles in the Horn of Africa all reduce the number of tourists.
- Negative publicity about wildlife conservation in Africa has given the wrong impression. Some think that poaching has destroyed those animals which the tourists most want to see.
- The number of expatriate residents in neighbouring countries has declined.
- The spread of the deadly disease AIDS has reduced the number of visitors because they are concerned for their health.
- The Gulf War of 1991 stopped all but essential travelling. As a result tourist resorts were empty for a few months.

Socio-Economic Problems of Tourism
Many of the things which bring wealth to our nation, also destroy other valuable aspects of our lifestyle. Some negative effects are as follows.

Western styles of behaviour have eroded our social etiquette and African traditions. For example, our traditional attitudes of respect towards elders and modest greetings have suffered.

Some people attempt to change their skin and hair colour. Although the natural colouring is suitable to this climate, they wish to appear similar to tourists from overseas. The effects of such changes can be extremely harmful.

Fashions that may be acceptable to cultures elsewhere, are often repugnant to societies in Africa, for example, the wearing of shorts and bikinis. For Kenyans fashion should be suitable for the culture of the wearer and respectful of accepted attitudes.

A man in our culture does not normally use drugs, cigarettes and alcohol until well into middle age. However this practice has spread to all age-groups, sexes and social groups through contact with the outside world. Much anti-social behaviour such as fighting, thieving and murder can be attributed to these harmful substances.

Strategies and Future Prospects of Tourism
Overall, the socio-economic benefits of tourism to Kenya outweigh the negative effects. However, tourism is a problematic industry; we cannot assume that it will continue to grow and prosper. Countries world-wide compete fiercely to attract tourists. In order to stay competitive, the tourist industry in Kenya needs to consider the following points.

Political stability is essential for healthy tourism. Regional co-operation, is also very important.

We must keep tourist facilities up to international standards. To do this we must constantly improve hotel and lodge accommodation; access roads to national parks and reserves; air, road and train links; telecommunications; health care and security.

We must take effective measures to conserve our resources and environment. These measures must control poaching of wildlife and marine specimens, and maintain suitable habitats. In this way the animal life may live and grow without stress. As wildlife is the basis of our tourism, this is vital.

We need to develop cultural centres in rural areas where tourists will meet rural people and admire their culture in a more dignified manner. Such development will stop the exploitation of both local people and tourists. In addition it will spread the economic benefits of tourism more widely.

To spread tourists more widely, we need to develop areas of Kenya which are not so well known. Educationalists need to increase the education programmes about how wildlife should be treated. This will give the visitor and Kenyan a better understanding of wildlife conservation.

Employees need high level manpower training. Such training will give them professional skills in wildlife and environmental conservation, as well as management of catering and recreation facilities .

Tour operators sometimes allow leakages of foreign exchange. Proper auditing supervision would help stop such dishonest practices. In addition if locally produced goods are promoted, this will stop the unnecessary importation of luxury goods. Such promotion will also increase the market for locally available raw materials.

We need to increase our tourism promotion in the main overseas cities. This will help to attract a constant flow of visitors to our beautiful country.

GROWTH OF INTERNATIONAL TOURISM TO KENYA
1946 - 1991

Year	No. of Visitors (in thousands)	Tourist Revenue (in K pound millions)
1946	16.09	-
1956	40.46	4.20
1966	106.52	12.10
1976	424.20	41.10
1986	604.00	250.00
1989	730.00	432.00
1990	801.00	530.00
1991	804.60	594.00
		(Ksh 11.880 billion)

INTERNATIONAL VISITORS TO KENYA BY COUNTRY OR REGION OF RESIDENCE
1980 - 1986
(in thousands)

Country of Residence	1980	1982	1984	1985	1986
W. Germany	78	67	76	100	112
United Kingdom	49	47	54	66	73
U.S.A.	30	35	43	54	60
Switzerland	28	29	32	45	49
Italy	22	23	26	34	38
France	16	18	19	25	27
Scandinavia	11	9	13	13	15
Canada	5	6	7	8	9
Asia	27	27	32	39	44

Source: Central Bureau of Statistics.

LOCAL AND INTERNATIONAL VISITORS
IN PARKS AND RESERVES
1976 - 1987

Year	Parks	Reserves
1976	636,170	4,569
1980	755,314	27,326
1982	803,285	44,200
1984	907,422	39,549
1986	594,356	217,764
1987	826,256	246,517

Wildlife Clubs and Conservation Organisations

There are many non-government organizations that deal with wildlife conservation. Most of them support research on wildlife, help with educational publications and workshops and provide equipment. They also undertake such conservation projects as anti-poaching operations, community conservation, veterinary support and animal rescue programmes. All such organisations are based in Nairobi.

So that you can contact them directly, here is a list of the names and addresses of these Wildlife Clubs and Conservation Organisations.

African Fund for Endangered Wildlife (AFEW)
Post Office Box 15004, Nairobi, Kenya Tel: 891658

African Wildlife Foundation (AWF)
Post Office Box 48177, Nairobi, Kenya Tel: 710367 Fax: 710372

East African Wild Life Society (EAWLS)
Post Office Box 20110, Nairobi, Kenya Tel: 748170 Fax: 746868

Elsa Wild Animal Appeal (EWAA)
Post Office Box 30029, Nairobi, Kenya Tel: 441344 Fax: 448966
Elsamere: Post Office Box 1497, Naivasha, Kenya.

Friends of Conservation (FOC)
Post Office Box 74901, Nairobi, Kenya Tel: 339537 Fax: 332873

International Union for Conservation of Nature (IUCN)
Post Office Box 68200, Nairobi, Kenya Tel: 502650 Fax: 608026

Rhino Ark
Post Office Box 30725, Nairobi, Kenya Tel: 741965/6 Fax: 740721

United Nations Environment Programme (UNEP)
Post Office Box 30552, Nairobi, Kenya Tel: 230800 Fax: 226890

Wildlife Clubs of Kenya (WCK)
Post Office Box 20184, Nairobi, Kenya Tel: (02) 891903 Fax: (02) 891906

Wildlife Conservation International (WCI)
Post Office Box 62844, Nairobi, Kenya Tel: 221699 Fax: 215969

World Wide Fund for Nature (WWF)
Post Office Box 62440, Nairobi, Kenya Tel: 332966 Fax: 332878

Discover the beauty of Kenya's natural and wildlife heritage!

Index of Developed National Parks, Reserves & Tourist Areas

CHAPTER 8

The National Parks, Reserves and Other Tourist Areas

The National Parks, Reserves, and other tourist areas in Kenya are presented within five areas of the country: The Nairobi, Rift Valley and Western Circuit; The Central and Northern Circuit; The Southern and Coastal Circuit; The North Coast; and The South Coast.

The Nairobi, Rift Valley and Western Circuit

NAIROBI NATIONAL PARK (117 sq km) *See map on page 106*

Nairobi National Park is located ten kilometres south-west of the Nairobi city centre. It is in an area which has a dry-season concentration of wildlife unsurpassed elsewhere in the country. It was originally part of the Great Southern Game Reserve created in 1900, but remained a grazing ground for Maasai and Somali herdsmen until the threat of the First World War intensified. It then became a training ground for the King's African Rifles. Unfortunately this resulted in serious destruction of both habitat and wildlife. In December,1946 the area was declared a National Park, the first in East Africa.

The Park has three main vegetational zones:

 a. Forest at the western end.

 b. Mbagathi-Athi riverine forest to the south.

 c. Grassy plains over most of the Park with scattered bush, riverine woodland, gorges and patchy reeds and sedges fringing man-made dams.

Over 100 species of mammals and 400 species of birds have been recorded in the park. It is always a source of amazement to the visitor that such a variety of wildlife can be viewed within sight of the skyscrapers and international airport of Nairobi. Four of 'the big five' can be found here: leopard, lion,

73

buffalo and rhino, (not elephant). During the rainy seasons (March through May and November through December) many of the grazers, especially wildebeest, Coke's hartebeest (*kongoni*), and zebra undergo a seasonal migration southwards through the Kitengela Game Conservation Area and Athi plains. Some predators such as lion and hyaena often follow the migrants. For the rest of the year the animals in the park remain near the artificial dams, and concentrations of over 25,000 animals can be found in the park at the driest times of the year with wildebeest, zebra and *kongoni* dominating.

Even when these herds have dispersed southwards in the rainy season, the park is rich with resident populations of buffalo, Maasai giraffe, black rhino, eland, impala, Grant's and Thomson's gazelle, common and Defassa waterbuck, bushbuck, bush duiker, steinbok, Kirk's dik dik, Bohor reedbuck, hippo, warthog, olive baboon, monkeys and a variety of carnivores, lion, spotted hyena, cheetah, leopard, jackals, bat-eared fox and many smaller carnivores. The bird life is always plentiful and their numbers are increased by a variety of migrants from Europe from March through May.

A short, self-guided nature trail along the Athi River on the Southern boundary, provides the visitor with an opportunity to watch hippo, crocodile, monkeys, terrapin and a great variety of birds.

Because of its proximity to a large urban centre, the Park has taken the opportunity to exploit the educational resources available.

Entrance to the Animal Orphanage at Nairobi National Park

At the Park's main gate is the Animal Orphanage, built in 1963 to care for the young animals which have either lost their mothers from predation, through poaching or natural causes. It also cares for wounded animals found abandoned by their herds in the bush. It has become a park within a park, offering a spectacle of big cats and other animals not indigenous to Kenya, often donated by other countries. An animal clinic has been built at the Orphanage for the treatment of sick and wounded animals. After treatment, the mature orphans or healed animals are often 'released' back into the wild.

A Wildlife Conservation Education Centre has been erected near the Main Gate to the park. This offers orientation lectures on wildlife and conservation to schools and colleges and members of the general public to arouse their awareness of the country's flora and fauna, and generate appreciation and support for their conservation. The centre also organises educational tours for VIPs. Free wildlife films are shown on week-days and at weekends from 2 - 4 pm. There is a reference library and a small museum.

A Wildlife Extension Service Unit was established in 1982 as part of the Education Centre and officers move out to the game concentrated areas outside the National Parks where they organize seminars and workshops for the local ranchers and farmers to discuss and find solutions to their problems and conflicts with wild animals. A Mobile Film Unit goes out to the rural areas to give wildlife conservation film shows and lectures. Together these facilities play an important part in providing recreation and wildlife conservation education for the country, as is shown by the 200,000 visitors per year.

OLORGESAILLIE PRE - HISTORIC SITE

This is a 50 acre pre-historic site of Middle Pleistocene Age about 70 km from Nairobi on the Magadi Road. There is a museum with stone age tools and fossilized remnants of extinct mammals first discovered in 1919 by J.W. Gregory, the eminent geologist. Later discoveries have revealed some parts of ancient camps and dwelling sites and these are displayed in the museum. A great variety of birds and some game can be viewed in the surrounding country.

LAKE MAGADI

Lake Magadi can be found just over 100 km from Nairobi, to the extreme south of the country. It is the most alkaline of all Kenyan Rift Valley lakes. The lake covers over 100 sq.km and the concentrated salts make it look white.

Temperatures there can reach over 100° F or 38° C. Surrounding the main lake basin are a number of hot springs with alkaline waters coming out of the ground at a temperature of about 113° F or 45° C. The spring waters flow into a central pan where intensive evaporation leaves behind a thick white deposit of slush. This slush contains a large amount of potassium, salts and other chemicals. It is the most prolific mineral source in the country and the Magadi Soda Company has been mining mineral salts there since the First World War.

The southern end of the lake is rich in bird life with flamingo, waders and some European migrants.

THE GREAT RIFT VALLEY

The Great Rift Valley runs for some 8,700 kms (5,400 miles) from the Jordan Valley in the Middle East to the Indian Ocean at Beira near the Zambezi River. It runs through the whole of the Red Sea before cutting through Ethiopia, Kenya, Tanzania, Mozambique. The section of the Valley in Kenya is also known as "Gregory Rift". It is dotted with recent volcanoes, like Mt. Longonot (partly extinct), Suswa, Eburu, Menegai, Londiani, Kakorinyo, and the central and northern islands in Lake Turkana. The section also contains seven lakes, none of which have an outlet: Lake Turkana (the Jade Sea), Baringo, Bogoria, Nakuru, Elementaita, Naivasha and Lake Magadi.

When it rains on the Rift Valley escarpments and on the surrounding countryside, water runs down rivers and streams to the lake basins. Water escapes from these lakes mainly through the high rate of evaporation. The evaporation leaves behind large quantities of salts and minerals which can be collected.

LAKE NAIVASHA (170 sq km) and MOUNT LONGONOT NATIONAL PARK (52 sq km) *See map of the latter on page 107*

About an hour's drive from Nairobi lies the fresh water Lake Naivasha at about 1890 metres above sea level. The road to the region climbs over the eastern escarpment giving spectacular views of the Rift Valley before descending towards the lake. The amazing variety of both aquatic and terrestrial bird life around Lake Naivasha is one of its main tourist attractions. Over 340 bird species have been spotted in a single visit! Other wildlife species in the area include buffalo, zebra, giraffe, eland, Chanler's reedbuck, *kongoni*, gazelles, and hippo. Trips across the lake to "Crescent

Island" are well worth the time and one can stroll among the wildlife and watch the fishermen in their small boats.

Pelicans and other water birds abound on Lake Naivasha

The lake's views are dominated by the shadow of **Mt Longonot** at 2,777 metres (9,109 ft), a partly extinct volcano which in 1983 was declared a national park. Between Mt. Longonot and Lake Naivasha stands **Njorowa Gorge or Hell's Gate** as it is often known. This provides exciting rock climbs and an impressive rock formation called Fischer's Tower. This area forms Hells Gate National Park (68 sq km), also established for the protection of various species of plains game and the rarest of Kenya's vultures, the Lammergeyer.

Olkaria Geothermal Power Station is 30 minutes away by road. It was built in 1981 on the edge of the National Park. 14 wells have been drilled in the volcanically active Olkaria Ridges to tap the gaseous steam from underground. The steam drives turbines to produce electricity, producing some 40 megawatts or 16% of all electricity produced in the country. Kenya is one of only 18 countries in the world to use geothermal energy.

KARIANDUSI PRE-HISTORIC SITE

On the way to Nakuru you pass the Kariandusi Pre-historic site which was discovered by Dr. Louis Leakey in 1928 and excavated between 1929 and 1947. In the museum are exhibited a number of stone-age objects. These include hand axes, obsidian or black volcanic glass knives and a molar of the straight-tusked elephant which once existed in England and the rest of Europe before it became extinct. Diatomite was also mined here and once used as face paint by the Maasai. Today it is used mainly for paints and insulation.

HYRAX HILL PRE - HISTORIC SITE

This is another prehistoric site in the Nakuru District. Here visitors can see pottery, hand axes, beads, obsidian tools, pestles, and re-constructed Iron-Age villages and dwellings. A cemetery shows the pre-historic methods of burial.

LAKE NAKURU NATIONAL PARK (188 sq km) *See map on page 108*

Lake Nakuru National Park lies immediately south of Nakuru town. In 1960 it became the first bird sanctuary in Africa and in 1967 it became a National Park. A unique euphorbia forest (*Euphorbia candelabrum*), stands on the eastern edge of the lake. This forest is said to be the largest single euphorbia forest in Africa. Areas of sedge, reeds, marsh and wooded grasslands, interspersed by rocky cliffs, surround the lake.

The lake is shallow and alkaline. This provides ideal conditions for the growth of microscopic blue algae which is the first link in the food chain. It provides sustenance for one to two million lesser flamingo, making the lake one of the greatest bird spectacles on earth. Flocks of 300,000 can be seen at one go. The flamingo population fluctuates from year to year as they migrate up and down the Rift Valley to find which lake has the best source of food. Even when the flamingo population is relatively low, there are still a huge number of other birds to be seen.

Tilapia *grahami* lives in the lake and feeds on the blue algae. It is a popular fish with both humans and birds. It attracts cormorants, spoonbills and pelicans. It is possible to drive right round the lake and stop at the bird watching hides along the northern shore.
Over 30 black and white rhino exist in the Park, which has been declared a rhino sanctuary.

MAASAI MARA NATIONAL RESERVE (1,672 sq km) *See map on page 109*

Maasai Mara National Reserve lies 275 km west of Nairobi at an altitude of 1650 metres (5,210 ft). It forms part of the Serengeti-Mara ecosystem. It has existed as a game conservation area since 1889 when it was part of the large Southern Game Reserve . In 1974 it was confirmed as Maasai Mara Game Reserve. Two rivers, the Mara and the Talek cross the grassland plains, and riverine woodland follows the river courses. The hills in the south-east end of the Reserve are covered with forest.

A huge variety of plains game are food for predators, lion, leopard, cheetah, hyaena, wild dog, jackals. Scores of hippo and crocodile live in the Mara River, which is frequently flooded during the rains. The Mara is rich in resident game with over 95 species recorded and a plentiful range of over 480 species of bird life.

The most spectacular attraction of the park is the annual mass migration of nearly two million wildebeest and zebra. From July to early October, the herds travel from the Serengeti National Park in Tanzania to the Maasai Mara Reserve. They turn northwards before reaching Lake Victoria, and cross the Mara River into Kenya looking for fresh pastures. At the beginning of the short rains in October, the herds turn south-east across the Olduvai Gorge and in January and February they migrate back to the Serengeti.

It was at Olduvai Gorge where Dr. Louis Leakey discovered the bones of wildebeest some two million years old. They were found alongside bones of early man, proving that this migrational route has existed for millions of years. Thousands of the migrating animals fall prey to the predators who follow the herds. Many more die in the Mara floods while crossing the river, but this is all a part of the natural pattern of 'survival of the fittest'.

RUMA NATIONAL PARK (120 sq km)

Ruma National Park is situated 197 km from Kisumu town and 32 km from Homa Bay. The park is only 30 km from the shore of Lake Victoria. It was established as a Game Reserve in 1966 mainly to protect the roan antelope, although many other species of game can also be found there including Jackson's hartebeest and topi.

Near Kisumu town is the **Kisumu Heronry,** first recorded in 1901 but officially protected in 1976. It is a bird sanctuary where over a thousand water-associated birds gather to breed from March to July.

Rusinga Island is reached by road or steamship from Homa Bay It is an archaeological site for the 17 million year old fossil remains of the early ape, Proconsul.

Ndere Island National Park (4 sq km) lies 13 km across the lake from Kisumu town. Herds of impala are the main attraction here. In addition it is crowded with bird life and there are magnificent lake views. Access is through Kisumu town or through the Kit Mikayi rocks and caves.

KAKAMEGA FOREST NATIONAL RESERVE (44.9 sq km)

This is believed to be one of the most important single indigenous forests south of the Sahara. It is a remnant of the true tropical rain forest which once spread from the River Congo basin and covered East and Central Africa. It is now reserved to preserve the forest and the unique West African type of animals, mammals, reptiles, birds and butterflies.

Elgon teak, red stinkwood, African satinwood and *musizi* are just some of the indigenous trees to be found here. The the rare red-tailed monkey, the De Brazza monkey, the potto and the rare yellow-backed duiker and the great blue turaco can also be found here. Due to its unique flora and fauna, the forest has become an area of special study for natural history students from all over the world.

MOUNT ELGON NATIONAL PARK (169 sq km) *See map on page 110*

Mount Elgon is the second highest mountain in Kenya. It is the remains of an extinct volcano whose central peak sunk under volcanic pressure. This formed a depression called a caldera. At the floor of the caldera are hot springs. Water from these springs flows eastwards forming the Suam River. The river cuts the eastern ridges and forms deep gorges with steep cliffs. It forms the Kenya-Uganda border and then flows eastwards to form the Turkwell river which finally flows into Lake Turkana.

The highest peak of the range, the Wagagai (4,320 mt; 14,178 ft) is in Uganda. In Kenya the highest is the Sudek peak (4,309 mt; 14,140 ft). **Koitoboss Rock** forms one of the main attractions in the park.

The savanna woodland on the south eastern slopes merge into thick mountain forests. Here one finds exciting caves which are frequented by elephant, buffalo, duiker and bushbuck who come here to lick salt from the cave walls. Leopard and hyena are also found hiding in the crevasses of the caves which provide perfect ambush habitat. There are also thousands of bats and rock hyrax in the caves.

A spotted hyena

80

At the upper levels, thick bamboo thickets grow amongst the mountain forests. These gradually merge into Cedar-Hagenia forest before the Afro-Alpine moorland where several forms of heather grow. Beyond the heather-zone to the top of the mountain is a region of high rocky peaks and rugged rocky slopes. The ground is covered with many flowering herbs.

It is possible to drive up to 12,000 ft. Walkers can then hike across moorlands to Koitoboss peak or climb over the crater rims and down the crater walls to the floor of the caldera. Many species of monkey, as well as a huge variety of birds, live in the mountain forests.

SAIWA SWAMP NATIONAL PARK (2 sq km)

The Saiwa Swamp National Park is situated 26 km east of Kitale town. In 1972 the park was created for the protection of the rare sitatunga antelope which lives in the swamp waters and the belt of rainforest. It is the only spot in the country where sitatunga can be seen with relative ease. Over one hundred sitatunga have been recorded and high observation points have been constructed for a better view of the swamps. It is the smallest National Park in Africa.

SOUTH TURKANA NATIONAL RESERVE (1,091 sq km) and NASOLOT NATIONAL RESERVE (92 sq km)

Visiting these reserves gives one a real taste for African adventure. They are in one of the most remote parts of the country. Visitors proceed along Kitale-Kapenguria-Lodwar Road. At Kapenguria District Commissioner's office visitors can see the famous cell of Kapenguria where the Freedom Fighter and the late President Mzee Jomo Kenyatta and his colleagues were remanded during the Kapenguria Trial of 1952/53. The cell has been preserved as a National Monument.

The reserves were established in 1979 for the preservation of the remaining wildlife species in the Turkana District. There is a limited number of forest and plains game. Nasolot has beautiful scenery overlooking the Turkwell Gorge. The reserves are only suitable for camping safaris as there is no accommodation within or nearby.

LAKE TURKANA (12,250 sq km; 9,350 sq km in Kenya)

Known as "The Jade Sea", Lake Turkana is the largest lake in Kenya. It is an inland sea in the middle of a desert, stretching northwards into Ethiopia. Several rivers from the Ethiopian Highlands flow down into its waters. Like other Rift Valley lakes, it has no outlet. The clear and unpolluted water is semi-alkaline but rich in fish, crocodile and bird life. Temperatures can rise to 145° F (63° C) which some visitors find rather warm!

Count Samuel Teleki Von Szek was the first white man to record seeing the lake in March, 1888. He named it Lake Rudolf in honour of his patron, the Austrian Archduke. The name was changed to Lake Turkana in 1975. Violent winds tear across the southern tip of the lake, forming high tides. This makes that part of the lake extremely dangerous for fishermen.

Giant Nile perch grow to over 200 lbs and have been known to weigh as much as 400 lbs, much to the delight of sporting fishermen. Tiger fish also give good sport, but commercial fishermen prefer to catch the Nile Tilapia. These fish are dried or frozen and marketed in Nairobi and elsewhere.

CENTRAL ISLAND NATIONAL PARK (5 sq km)

Central Island National Park is right in the middle of Lake Turkana. There is an active volcano which sometimes belches out clouds of sulphurous steam and smoke. It was established as a national park in 1983 to protect the breeding ground of the Nile crocodile. The island has three lakes; Crocodile Lake, Flamingo Lake and Tilapia Lake.

The El-Molo tribe inhabit two small islands in the south-eastern corner of the lake. The tribe was once reduced to only 80 individuals and described as the smallest tribe in Africa. In 1964 John Hillaby described them as *"the race that time had forgotten"* . The group has now multiplied to over 500 people who live on a protein rich diet of fish, crocodile, hippo, terrapin and birds.

Hippo graze at night

SOUTH ISLAND NATIONAL PARK (39 sq km)

South Island National Park is right at the centre of the El-Molo country. It was established in 1983 for the protection of the breeding ground of Nile Crocodile and hippos and the unique venomous snakes including the puff adder, cobra and sand vipers. The park can be reached through Loiyangalani (*a place of trees*) where the Oasis Lodge provides a base and facilities for travellers. From the lodge visitors can make bird-watching trips to the island or camping safaris to Mt. Kulal or Mt. Moiti.

LAKE BOGORIA NATIONAL RESERVE (107 sq km)

Lake Bogoria is about 80 km north of Nakuru town in the Great Rift Valley. Formerly known as Lake Hannington, this is one of the most beautiful of the Rift Valley lakes. It is a shallow soda lake which was established as a National Reserve in November, 1983. The reserve covers the whole lake and its surroundings. It is a geological wonder no-one can afford to miss. Jets of steam and boiling water shoot out of geysers and fumaroles (holes in the ground) indicating the sort of volcanic activities which created the Great Rift Valley a very long time ago.

When the water levels in Lake Nakuru become low. thousands of both lesser and greater flamingo migrate to Lake Bogoria. It is the best place in Kenya to see the greater kudu which live on the western shores of the lake.

LAKE BARINGO

Lake Baringo is a freshwater neighbour a little further north. There are schools of hippo and crocodile, but the major attraction of the lake is the multitude of birds. Over 400 species have been identified here. Gibraltar Island in the lake offers the largest colony of Goliath heron in East Africa. Bird watching trips and fishing safaris are organised for visitors by boat or on foot.

The Central and Northern Circuit

OL DONYO SABUK NATIONAL PARK (18 sq km) *See map on page 111*

Ol Donyo Sabuk means 'Sleeping Buffalo' in Maasai. It is also known as Kilima Mbogo or 'Hill of Buffalo' in Kiswahili. Situated about 80 km east of Nairobi, beyond Thika on the Thika-Garissa road, it was established as a national park in 1967. The forested slopes and high mountains offer outstanding beauty and wonderful views. On clear mornings visitors can see the snowy peaks of Mount Kenya over 100 km away. A nine kilometre motor track through the forest leads to the summit. Travellers can see the grave of Sir William Northrup McMillan, a wealthy American farmer, who was knighted for his services in the First World War.

A short distance before the entrance to the park are the beautiful **Fourteen Falls** on the Athi River. These drop impressively over a 27 metre (90 ft) slope.

ABERDARES NATIONAL PARK (970 sq km) *See map on page 112*

The Aberdares range lie 17 kilometres north-west of Nyeri town and about 100 km from Nairobi. Mt. Kenya and the Aberdares form the highest peaks of the Kenya Central Highlands. They are part of an ancient group of extinct volcanoes which rise to a height of 3,998 metres (13,120 ft). They are the country's major water catchment areas, and therefore of immense importance. Plans have been made to enclose the whole of the Aberdares Sanctuary with an electric fence (powered by a water wheel generator). This will include the entire indigenous rain forest and give a final fenced area of 970 sq km, approximately the size of 100,000 football pitches!

The Ark is set in the heart of the Aberdares National Park.

Let's Protect Kenya's Wildlife Heritage!

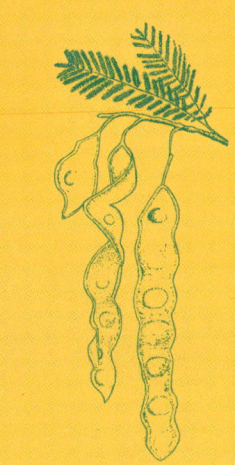

Beisa Oryx mostly inhabit arid brush and scrub lands north of the Tana River

Cheetah mother is on the watch as her cub pauses for a quiet drink

Serval cats hunt alone, are mainly nocturnal and can climb trees

Lion stop for a cool drink
in the heat of the African sun

Lion roam the plains of Amboseli National Park
at the foot of Mt. Kilamanjaro

A majestic Eland bull
on the grassy plains of
Nairobi National Park

Watching game from
a shady vantage point,
lions often hunt in groups,
surprising their prey by
well-planned attacks
from all sides

Warthogs like to wallow in muddy
places but at night slide into deep
holes ready to use their tusks in
self-defense

Ostrich eggs kept warm by the sun

The Burchell's zebra is a common sight on the open plains of Kenya

The male lion's role is to protect the pride and patrol their territory. In return, they take the "lion's share" of any prey the females bring back from the hunt

The spotted Hyena is a scavenger and skillful hunter. Only the spotted and rare striped hyena are found in Kenya

The range's eastern slopes are covered with thick forests. At higher altitudes there is the bamboo-hagenia zone. Here trees are hung with long strands of lichen or 'old-man's beard' and multitudes of ferns, mosses and orchids grow along their trunks and branches. Like the rest of East Africa's mountains, the moorlands are covered with a special kind of vegetation called Afro-Alpine. This consists of giant forms of heath, groundsels and senecio which grow above the forest belt. Clear streams form numerous rivers which flow over a series of waterfalls. The **Guru water Falls** dominate the scene.

The extremely shy and rare bongo lives in the higher bamboo zone.   A variety of common forest zone mammal species can also be seen, among them elephant, buffalo, rhino, giant forest hog, bushbuck, black and white colobus monkey, both African and Palm civets, spotted hyena and porcupine. The two lodges in the Aberdares, the Ark and Treetops are specifically designed to view the animals after dark. Both have flood-lit salt licks and water holes which can be easily seen from the lodge balconies.

MOUNT KENYA NATIONAL PARK (715 sq km)

Mt. Kenya, or Kirinyaga (black and white striped mountain) is the sacred mountain of the Gikuyu people where their god *"Ngai "* is believed to live. It is a giant extinct volcano. The ridges have now been worn down, leaving only the central peaks. Mount Kenya is the second highest mountain in Africa (next to Mt Kilimanjaro in Tanzania), and the only spot in the world where snow is found on the Equator.

The first white man to see and record seeing snow on Mt Kenya was the German missionary, Ludwig Krapf in December, 1849. Few people believed his reports until Joseph Thomson confirmed the sight in 1883. In 1899 the Englishman, Sir Halford Mackinder conquered Batian the mountain's highest peak, at 5,199 metres (17,058 ft). The first known African to reach the top was Kisoi Munyao in 1959. In 1963 he raised the flag of the newly independent Kenya on the summit of the mountain.

The park protects and preserves large sections of mountain forests and bamboo thickets with their varied wildlife, the alpine moorlands, glaciers, tarns and glacial moraines. Ascending the mountain, one crosses several different zones of vegetation:

Lower Montane Forest (between 2,100 to 2,400 metres) Main tree species include Camphor (*Ocotea*), Cedar (*Juniperus*), Olive (*Olea*) and Podo (*Podocarpus*).

Bamboo Zone (2,400 to 2,800 metres) The giant grass bamboo grows as a forest attaining heights of 12-15 metres and there are many flowering herbs.

Hagenia/hypericum zone (2,850 to 3,000 metres) This is high altitude rain forest with patches of bamboo thickets and open glades. Dominant trees include Rosewood (*Hagenia*), Giant St. John's Worts (*Hypericum*), Lobelia. The trees are hung with long strands of lichen, ferns, mosses and orchids. The rare Bongo may also be seen in this zone.

The Heath Zone (3,000 to 3,500 metres) This is open moorland of tussock grass mixed with other plants which vary with altitude. Giant senecio, Lobelia, Giant groundsel and fields of everlasting flowers make the area particularly attractive.

The Alpine Zone (3,500 to 4,350 metres) This is the true mountain region of high rock peaks, tarns and rugged rocky slopes. Senecio's mass flowering occurs only once in every twenty or more years, the most recent occurring in 1978-79. Lobelia species are found in family groups along wet valley bottoms. The ground is covered with many flowering herbs.

Nival Zone (4,350 metres to the top of the mountain). This is the zone of rock and ice. Slopes are mostly bare gravel and scree left by glaciers. Colourful lichens are the common plant form at this altitude. The composite Senecio (*keniophytum*) is found a few metres from the glaciers. Helichrysum (*brownei*) occurs on all the peaks in cracks of weathered rocks. The main central peaks, Batian, Nelion and Lenana are the central cores of volcanic cones. Their rims have been worn down, leaving the peaks sticking out. Point Lenana at 4,970 metres (16,355 ft) is more suitable for climbers with little experience. Peaks Batian and Nelion require ropes, ice-axes and other specialised equipment.

Climbing Routes: Intending climbers should be informed of the dangers of cold and snow blindness, sharp rocks and crevasses. Above all, beware of the possibility of pulmonary oedema, a dangerous lung congestion which affects climbers at 3,950 metres (13,000 ft) and above. Climbers are advised to get acclimatized before attempting the climb. Consult the **Mountain Club of Kenya** P.O. Box 45741, Nairobi, for additional information. Visitors intending to climb or stay on the mountain for a long time must be accompanied by guides and porters. In case of trouble while on the mountain, there is a Mountain Rescue Team organized and run by the Mt. Kenya National Park.

Mount Kenya, or Kirinyaga, is the ancestral home of the Gikuyu people.

Naro-Moru Route: This is the quickest route. From the Park Headquarters the motor track continues for 10 km to the Meteorological Station at 3,050 metres (10,000 ft). Here there is a ranger post, a self-service lodge for 30 people, a porters' dormitory and a parking area.

Sirimon Motor Track: This is the easiest route to reach the moorland, but it requires a four-wheel drive vehicle. Climbers pass through juniper and podo forest before reaching the bamboo zone. Elephant, buffalo, bushbuck and bush duiker and sometimes the bongo or leopard can be seen along this route. Motorists can drive up to 3,930 metres (12,900 ft) where there is a campsite near a stream.

Timau Track: This motor track on the northern slopes of the mountain enables the visitor to drive up to 4,160 metres (13,640 ft).

Chogoria Route: On the eastern slopes of the mountain.

MERU NATIONAL PARK (870 sq km) *See map on page 113*

Meru National Park lies 85 km east of Meru town in the north-eastern lowlands, below the Nyambeni Hills. It was established as a County Council Game Reserve in 1957. It is a low lying park on a semi-arid zone with average temperatures of 70°F. There is irregular rainfall of 300 to 360 mm on the east to 640 to 760 mm on the west. The western section is a hilly upland of volcanic rocks with rich black volcanic or cotton soils. It is drained by 15 permanent streams. The eastern section is an open plain of red lateritic soils. Several hills of pre-cambrian rocks, namely the Mugwango hills, Leopard Rocks and Gutich, tower above the surrounding plains.

There are 15 streams and seasonal luggas which flow into the main rivers, the Rojerwero, Murera and Ura. These eventually converge into Kenya's mightiest river, the Tana. The rivers are fringed by dense riverine forest or stands of Doum and Raffia palms. Combretum woodland prevails in the western section of the park, with bush and acacia commiphora woodland dominating the south and south-eastern sections. Several swamps found in the Murera, Mulika, Bwatherongi, Mugwango and Leopard Rock areas. During the dry seasons, when the rest of the park is scorched, these swamps become the centre of wildlife concentrations.

The park has a road system of over 600 km which gives pleasant drives for game viewing. It is popularly known as "Elsa country", a tribute to Joy Adamson who reared the orphan lioness Elsa and later rehabilitated her into the wild. Wildlife is plentiful and varied.

Meru Park was the only park in the country where, until recently, white rhinos lived. They were re-introduced there in 1966 after fossil evidence showed that the species existed in the area many centuries ago. The name "white rhino" is a corruption of the Afrikaans word for 'wide'. This refers to their wide lips as opposed to the pointed prehensile lips of the Black rhino.

The white rhino has a wide top lip

A circuit of 19 km (12 miles) along the Tana River enables the visitor to see hippo, crocodile and a variety of other animals along the river banks. Before

88

the Tana joins the Rojerwero river, it flows over a constricted rocky gorge causing the spectacular **Adamson Falls.**

This is one of the best parks to see cheetah and lion. Birds too are plentiful. Access routes are varied:

- Nairobi Embu route (320 km), entering at Ura Gate.

- Nairobi-Nanyuki-Meru route (370 km) entering at Murera Gate

- Meru-Mulika Lodge Airstrip.

SAMBURU, BUFFALO SPRINGS and SHABA NATIONAL RESERVES
See maps on pages 114, 115and 116 respectively

The three reserves lie about 325 km from Nairobi and 50 km from Isiolo town on the Isiolo-Marsabit road. Samburu and Buffalo Springs were separated in 1963. The land on the Samburu side was established as a Game Reserve (255 sq km) under the Samburu County Council. The Isiolo section (339 sq km) was similarly established under the Isiolo County Council. These two reserves, plus the newly established **Shaba National Reserve** (239 sq km) lie on the ecological zone with a hot and dry climate during the day and are cool at night. There is a maximum annual mean temperature of 30° C and a minimum of 18° C - 22° C. The annual average rainfall is between 255-510 mm.

The Samburu and Buffalo Springs are traversed by the Uaso Nyiro river. The beautiful scenery and wildlife along the banks of this river are some of its major attractions. The strips of riverine forest, thickets and clusters of tall feathery **Doum palms** create a lively habitat for many species, particularly primates .

The Shaba National Reserve was established in 1974. The Great North Road from Isiolo to Marsabit separates it from the other two reserves. The three form the Samburu/Isiolo Complex, a trio of beautiful game sanctuaries, unsurpassed anywhere in the country. Shaba got its name from a cone of volcanic rock in the reserve. It was here that the ageing Joy Adamson prepared to release Penny, the orphaned leopard cub found near her Lake Naivasha home. Penny, "the Queen of Shaba" was almost ready to be released into the bush. On the evening of 3rd January, 1980 Joy went for her usual evening stroll: she never returned. Her body was later discovered on a bush track, the victim of a brutal murder that shocked the world.

MARALAL GAME SANCTUARY

Maralal is the administrative centre of Samburu District. The Samburu people who inhabit this beautiful part of the country are close relatives of the tall, nomadic Maasai of southern Kenya. They are a splinter group which broke away from the Nilotic Maasai during their southerly migrations down the River Nile in the 16th century. The beautifully ornamented morans (warriors) march fearlessly across the plains.

Maralal Safari Lodge lies about two and a half kilometers from the town. It overlooks a water hole where animals gather to drink. The lodge organizes trips to a hill in the sanctuary where visitors get a good opportunity to watch leopards from the safety of a hide. Also in Maralal is the tin-roofed bungalow, (now a National Monument) where Mzee Jomo Kenyatta was detained in 1961. On his release he led Kenya to Independence in 1963. A rough, rocky track runs from Maralal town over and across Lopet Plateau. It leads to Lake Turkana, via Baragoi, to Loiyangalani on the shores of the lake.

LOSAI NATIONAL RESERVE (1,806 sq km)

This reserve lies almost half way between Marsabit and Isiolo. It was founded in 1976 for the protection of the wildlife. This reserve is suitable for camping safaris for those who like to camp in unspoilt and remote, semi-arid parts of the country.

MARSABIT NATIONAL PARK and RESERVE *See map on page 117*
(Total=1,558 sq km: Park 360 sq km and Reserve 1,198 sq km)

Mt Marsabit lies about 560 km from Nairobi by road. It is the most attractive of the extinct volcanic mountains of northern Kenya. Rising out of the northern desert wilderness like a green oasis, the mountain top is 1,707 metres (5,598 ft) above the desert floor. Its peak is covered with mist forests and several beautiful crater lakes like Sokorte Guda (Lake Paradise). Here buffalo and elephant congregate for water in the late afternoons. This was the home of Ahmed, a large tusked elephant who was protected by a Presidential Decree. He died of old age in January, 1974. A life-sized model of Ahmed and his skeleton and tusks are now on display at the Kenya National Museum in Nairobi. Ahmed's descendants are commonly seen.

Nomadic tribesmen, the Boran, Rendille and Gabbra, bring their cattle and camels from the desert to water in the 'Singing Wells' of the mountain springs.

It is the gateway to Sibiloi National Park and the Chalbi Desert which stretches to the eastern shores of Lake Turkana.

"Do you really think this will fool the tourists?"

SIBILOI NATIONAL PARK (1,570 sq km)

Sibiloi National Park is the most remote park in Kenya on the eastern shores of Lake Turkana. It lies about 960 km by road from Nairobi via Marsabit, and about 300 km from Marsabit town. It was established in 1973 for the preservation of the valuable archaeological sites found there, and the protection of the greatest crocodile concentration in the world. About 12,000 Nile crocodiles inhabit the lake waters, along with considerable numbers of hippo, tilapia, tiger fish, giant Nile perch, flamingo, waders and pelicans.

The Koobi Fora region is the home of the pastoral Gabra tribe and their livestock. It is also rich in fossil remains of animals (extinct elephant species) and human beings (*Homo Erectus*) dating back nearly three million years. It has been named the "Cradle of Mankind". In 1971, Bernard Ng'eno, a field worker in Dr. Richard Leakey's excavation team, discovered a skull fragment in the area. More fragments were collected from the sand and when the pieces were assembled they formed a brain case similar to that of *Homo Sapiens* or modern man.

Large areas of petrified (turned to stone) wood are the surviving remains of the great cedar forests. These once covered the lake shores about seven million years ago and indicate that there was once far greater rainfall than today. Access to Koobi Fora is by chartered aeroplane or along a motor track from Loiyangalani.

The Southern and Coastal Circuit

AMBOSELI NATIONAL PARK (392 sq km) *See map on page 118*

Formerly part of the huge Southern Game Reserve, Amboseli was made into a separate "Maasai Amboseli Game Reserve" in 1948. Under the Royal National Parks of Kenya Organisation in 1961 it was handed over to the Kajiado County Council.

Amboseli is the home of the Maasai people and they had previously lived together in harmony with the wildlife in the area. However there was over-grazing around the Amboseli swamplands, especially during the dry seasons. This threatened the future of Amboseli as a wildlife conservation area. The authorities feared that the expanding Maasai population and their livestock would overrun and destroy the attractions of Amboseli, so in 1974 they declared 392 sq km around the swamps as a National Park. The Maasai are now provided with adequate supplies of water outside the park for their livestock.

Amboseli is situated 250 km from Nairobi, at the foot of the highest mountain in Africa, **Mt. Kilimanjaro** (5,895 metres or 19,340 ft). It is mostly fairly dry with 160 mm falling in the rainy season (March through May) and 80 mm in the short rains (October to December). The western section of the park is an ancient lake bed which for most of the year is a dry, flat stretch but becomes flooded during the rainy season.

The Enkongo Narok and Ol Okenya swampy areas receive their waters from the snow-capped peaks of Mt. Kilimanjaro. The water travels underground and emerges on the plains as springs. These springs form the two swamps which sustain the wildlife and vegetation of Amboseli. Visitors to Amboseli always wonder how such a dry country can support such a large concentration of wildlife. This underground water supply to the swampy regions provides the answer. Elephants stand waist deep in the water and hippos love the deep pools. Today, Amboseli supports the widest variety of birds and wildlife in the country, so there is always plenty to see.

Part of the park is a dry open plain and excellent for spotting cheetah The other part has small hills and thorn-bush with scattered rocks of lava (from the volcano). Two mountains dominate the area; Ol Donyo Orok Hill and the immense Mt. Kilimanjaro, just across the border in Tanzania. The look-out point on Observation Hill offers wide views of the park and beyond.

Access to this area is by the following routes:

- From Nairobi via Athi River on the Kajiado-Namanga Road. Turn left at Namanga and go on to Meshanani Gate (240 km).

- From Nairobi following the Mombasa Road to Emali, on to the Loitokitok Road. Turn right after about 65 km and enter the Park via the Lemeiboti Gate (230 km).

- From Tsavo West National Park over the Chyulu Hills. Continue to Loitokitok and enter the Park via Olkelunyiet Gate.

TSAVO NATIONAL PARK (20,812 sq km) *See maps on pages 119 and 120*

Tsavo East and West National Parks: At the turn of the 19th century few people lived in the vast scrubland of the present Tsavo National Park. There were three reasons why people did not live there. Firstly, the land was barren; secondly the tsetse fly prevented cattle ranching; thirdly, frequent slave raids from the coast caused great insecurity in the area. Most of the land was left for wildlife to roam freely. When the railway was being constructed in 1898 there was a multitude of game, but slowly hunters moved in and began to destroy the wildlife.

In 1948 Tsavo National Park was established. It was the second wildlife sanctuary in Kenya and one of the largest in Africa. The park is about half-way between Nairobi and Mombasa and is divided by the road and railway line into East and West.

There is a famous story of the *"Man Eaters of Tsavo"* They were two lions which many people believed were not real animals but the spirits of two departed chieftains. They were thought to have taken on the shapes of lions in protest against the construction of the railway line through their land.

Lion and cub.

The two man-eating lions attacked the railway workmen for over nine months. Every night they attacked they succeeded in snatching a coolie or construction worker from the camp. They escaped any attempts to kill them and caused a reign of terror amongst the workforce. Eventually the entire construction work was stopped for four weeks when the workers refused to continue until the lions had been killed. Colonel Patterson, the officer in charge of railway construction, finally managed to shoot the lions which had killed a total of 28 people.

DO NOT GET OUT OF YOUR CAR -
their relatives may be watching out for you!

TSAVO WEST NATIONAL PARK (9,065 sq km) *See map on page 119*

The western section of **Tsavo West** is made up of recent (about 400 years old) volcanic lava flows. The lava mantles are called "Shetani" or the "Devil Mountains". They absorb rain water which then flows underground for 40 km and emerges as the **Mzima Springs**. These springs create a home for thousands of aquatic animals, especially hippo. The hippos are best observed from the safety of an underwater observation point which has been specially constructed to let the visitor see how they behave below the surface. After a series of pools, the water disappears underground again to emerge as Mzima River. It joins the Tsavo River 7 kms downstream.

In the extreme south-west area of the park is the beautiful **Lake Jipe**. The lake is fed by an underground water flow from the snow-capped peaks of Mount Kilimanjaro. It is a magnificent bird colony with Black heron and Pygmy geese dominating the scene. Migratory birds from the northern hemisphere flock towards the Ngulia escarpment and the Ngulia Hills (1820 metres or 5,974 ft) during the autumn. This makes the area of particular interest for anyone interested in bird life, and provides scientists with important information on the birds' migratory routes and habits.

TSAVO EAST NATIONAL PARK (11,747 sq km) *See map on page 120*

Tsavo East is an open, dry wilderness with almost the same flora and fauna as Tsavo West. The Yatta Plateau is one of the longest lava flows in the world and dominates the park. The Athi River provides the essential water. This river becomes the Galana in the middle of the park and then disappears through a narrow rocky gorge to emerge in the spectacular **Lugard's Falls**. The pools below the Falls are the home to a large number of crocodile who enjoy the sandy banks.

Mudanda Rock, between Voi and Manyani, provides a water-catchment area. A natural dam is formed where elephant and other game come to drink. An observation point above the dam provides visitors with a perfect spot to view the concentrations of game which frequent this dam. The **Aruba Dam** (85 hectares) is in the middle of the hot and waterless Taru Desert. It is the only permanent water hole in the park.

The elephant in Tsavo East have destroyed the acacia commiphora woodland. It has become scrub-type grassland which now attracts large populations of zebra and other plains game. Nearly all the bird species found in dry savanna-bush and woodland country are represented in Tsavo. The giant baobab trees, which may live as long as 1,000 years, are scattered widely. Each year, after the rains, the blossoming of the acacia trees and the desert roses are a major floral attraction.

The North Coast

MOMBASA MARINE NATIONAL PARK (10 sq km)

This new park was established in 1986. It lies about 13 kilometres from Mombasa town, across the road from the Hotel Intercontinental. It was created to protect the corals and coral fishes. The park is surrounded by a 200 sq km **Marine National Reserve** , where traditional fishing is allowed under licence.

Near Nyali the Bamburi Cement Company have developed a private wildlife and forest conservation sanctuary. It is established it in an old quarry from which the company had dug coral limestone to make cement. A Swiss agronomist, Rene Haller, helped the company to rehabilitate the devastated environment. Forests, shrubs, a vineyard, and areas of citrus, mangoes and bananas are grown. Ponds where many species of fish are bred all enhance the area. The **Kipepeo Aquarium,** with its coral gardens, shells and coral fish, is a further attraction of the Bamburi Quarry Farm.

ARABUKO - SOKOKE FOREST NATIONAL PARK and RESERVE

Located south of Watamu, six square kilometres of this forest has been declared a National Park . A remnant of the indigenous coastal forest, it was once famous for its rubber trees, avifauna and butterfly populations. It is now the only place in the country where the rare Aders Duiker and the Golden Rumped Elephant Shrew live. Unique bird species include the Sokoke Pipit and the Sokoke Scops Owl.

MALINDI and WATAMU MARINE NATIONAL PARKS and RESERVES

The national reserves enclose the two national parks. The landward boundary is 30 metres from the highest tide mark and they extend for about six kilometres out to sea.

WATAMU MARINE NATIONAL PARK (10 sq km)

Watamu Marine National Park lies 24 kilometres south of Malindi town. On the way visitors pass the famous "Kabwere Dispensary" where the Giriama Wizard keeps over 100 wives and sells potions and anti-witchcraft medicines. The most attractive feature of the park are the three caves at the entrance to **Mida Creek** on the southern boundary. When the tide is low, visitors can take a boat and see the 6 ft long, 200 kg giant groupers (*'Tewa'* in Kiswahili). Park authorities protect the area carefully and limit the number of visitors to the caves. Mida Creek is also an important bird watching area, especially from March to May.

The dry seasons (Jan to March and June to October) are the best time to visit these marine parks. During the rainy seasons the rains make the water too rough and the silt brought down by the rivers spoils the visibility over the reefs. Visitors are not allowed to fish, collect corals or shells; nor may they disturb or destroy the sensitive coral gardens.

MALINDI MARINE NATIONAL PARK

Malindi Marine National Park stands between Chanoni Point and Leopard Point. Casuarina Point is the Headquarters and entrance to the park. The north reef runs parallel to the shore. The sea bed is exposed at low tide, leaving many shallow pools filled with corals and fish. The southern section of the park is the home of the famous coral gardens. These are the most popular attraction for divers, snorkelers and visitors who view the fish from glass-bottomed boats.

On the shore side is the Barracuda Channel. Here holes and crevices in the corals are filled with Moray eels, Sergeant Major fish and Octopus. Green turtles lay their eggs and bury them in the beach above high water marks. Big game fish like Blue Marlin, Sailfish, Giant Grouper and Mako sharks are also seen in the reserves.

THE TANA RIVER PRIMATES NATIONAL RESERVE

The Tana River Primates National Reserve is found near Garsen on the Malindi/Lamu road. It was established to protect the **Red Colobus Monkey** and the **Crested Mangabey.** These two endangered primates only live in this particular area. As their habitat begins to decrease, the population of these monkeys is increasingly in danger.
Garsen is a trading centre for Somali, Orma and Pokomo tribesmen who trade in livestock, clothing and foodstuffs.

KIUNGA MARINE and DODORI NATIONAL RESERVE

225 kilometres north of Malindi is the newly established **Kiunga Marine National Reserve.** Here visitors can see the rare Dugong and the Green Turtle.

On the shores of the island in the **Dodori National Reserve** live the rare Hunter's antelope and the lesser kudu. The reserve is next to Kiunga.

The South Coast

KISITE - MPUNGUTI MARINE NATIONAL PARK (28 sq km)

The park lies about 120 kilometres from Mombasa. It was established in 1978 and offers the best snorkeling and diving sites. Shimoni, at the gateway to the park, was where thousands of slaves were kept in a huge cave while waiting to be shipped to Arabia. The cave can be visited.

Boat trips are organised from the Shimoni shoretown to one of the best deep-sea fishing areas, the Pemba channel, or to the **Kisite Marine National Park.** As visitors sail to the marine park they may see dolphins swimming alongside. Wasini Island has a unique moon-like landscapes and old Arab villages.

SHIMBA HILLS NATIONAL RESERVE (192 sq km) *See map on page 121*

This reserve lies about 40 km south of Mombasa. It consists of rolling hills of grasslands, alternating with beautiful patches of equatorial rain forest and sea views. It was established in 1968 for the protection of the last breeding herd of Sable antelope. Roan antelope, translocated from Ithanga Hills near Thika, may also be seen. Cooler than the coast, the reserve has panoramic views of the ocean to the south, and the Usambara and Pare mountains over in Tanzania.

Sable antelope in the Shimba Hills

National Parks

National Park	Size (sq km)	District	Year Gazetted
Aberdares	715	Nyeri	1950
Amboseli	392	Kajiado	1974
Arabuko-Sokoke	6	Kilifi	1991
Central Island	5	Turkana/Marsabit	1983
Chyulu	471	Machakos	1983
Hell's Gate	68	Nakuru	1984
Kora	1787	Tana River	1989
Lake Nakuru	188	Nakuru	1967
Longonot	52	Nakuru	1983
Malka Mari	876	Mandera	1989
Meru	870	Meru	1966
Mount Elgon	169	Trans-Nzoia	1968
Mount Kenya	715	Nyeri/Meru	1949
Nairobi	117	Nairobi	1946
Ndere Island	4	Kisumu	1986
Ol Donyo Sabuk	18	Machakos	1967
Ruma	120	South Nyanza	1983
Saiwa Swamp	2	Trans-Nzoia	1974
Sibiloi	1,570	Marsabit	1973
South Island	39	Marsabit	1983
Tsavo East	11,747	Taita Taveta/Kitui	1948
Tsavo West	9,065	Taita Taveta	1948

National Reserves

National Reserve	Size (sq km)	District	Year Gazetted
Arawale	533	Garissa	1974
Bisanadi	606	Isiolo	1978
Boni	1,339	Garissa	1976
Buffalo Springs	131	Isiolo	1963
Dodori	877	Lamu	1976
Kakamega	45	Kakamega	1985
Kamnarok	88	Baringo	1983
Kitui North	745	Kitui	1979
Kitui South	1,833	Kitui	1979
Laikipia	165	Laikipia	1991
Lake Bogoria	107	Baringo	1970
Losai	1,806	Marsabit	1976
Marsabit	1,558	Marsabit	1962
Maasai Mara	1,672	Narok	1974
Mwea	68	Embu	1976
Nasolot	92	West Pokot	1979
Ngai Ndethya	212	Machakos	1976
Rahole	1,270	Garissa	1976
Rimoi	66	Elgeyo Marakwet	1983
Samburu	165	Samburu	1963
Shaba	239	Isiolo	1974
Shimba Hills	192	Kwale	1968
S. Turkana	1,091	Turkana	1979
Tana River Primate	169	Tana River	1976

Marine Parks and Reserves

Marine Parks and Reserves	Size (sq km)	District	Year Gazetted
Malindi MNP	6	Kilifi	1968
Malindi MNR	213	Kilifi	1968
Mombasa MNP	10	Mombasa	1986
Mombasa MNR	200	Mombasa	1986
Kisite/Mpunguti MNP	28	Kwale	1978
Mpunguti MNR	11	Kwale	1978
Watamu MNP	10	Kilifi	1968
Watamu MNR	32	Kilifi	1968
Kiunga MNR	250	Lamu	1979

Sanctuaries

Sanctuary	Size (sq km)	District	Year Gazetted
Maralal	6	Samburu	1968

Selected Maps of Developed

National Parks and Reserves

Plus

A Visitor's Wildlife Chart

All maps courtesy of Wildlife Planning Unit 1992, G. Tokro & F. N. Muchiri, unless otherwise credited. Wildlife Chart by Jacaranda Designs, Ltd.

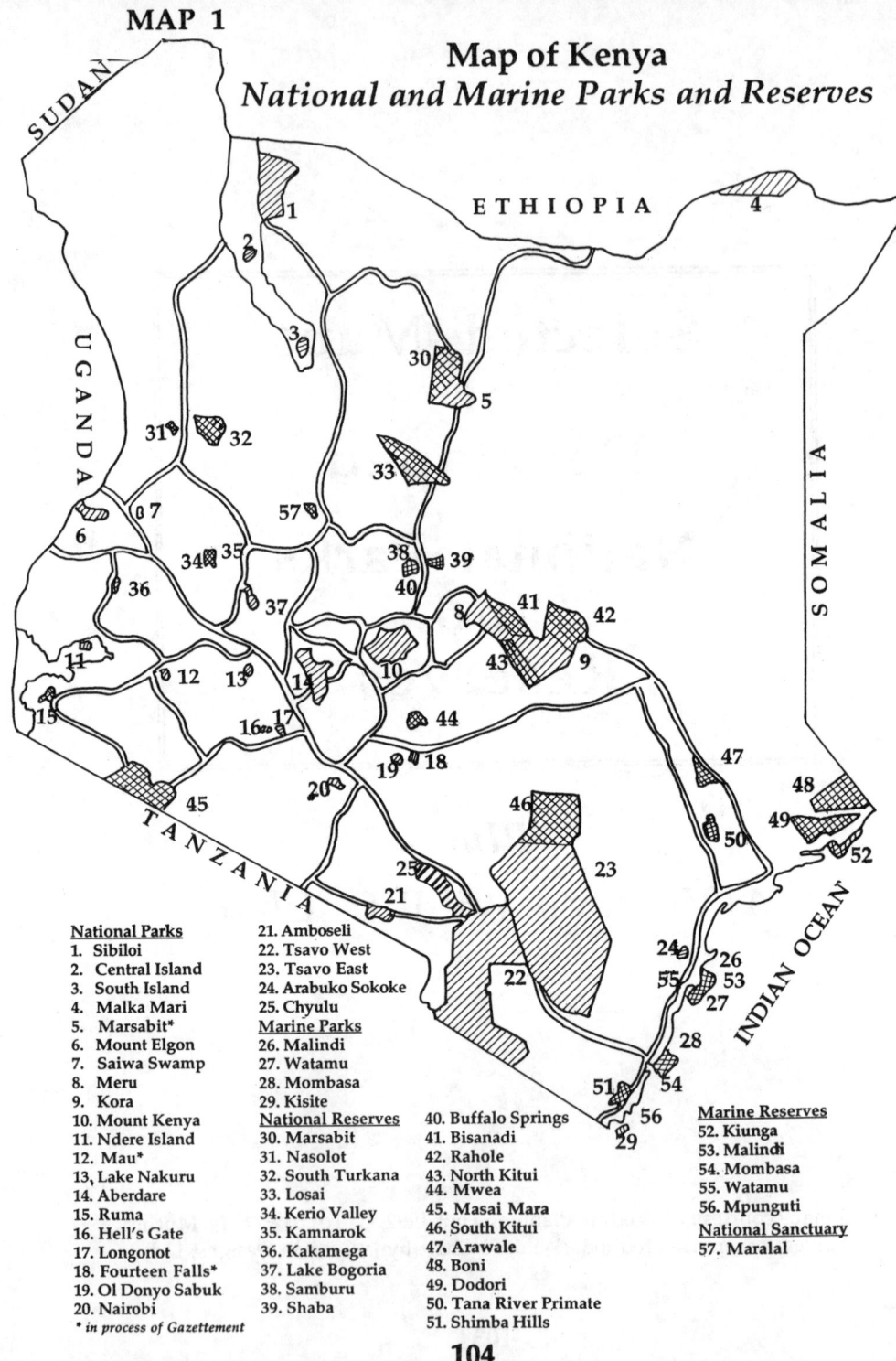

MAP 1

Map of Kenya
National and Marine Parks and Reserves

SUDAN

ETHIOPIA

UGANDA

SOMALIA

TANZANIA

INDIAN OCEAN

104

MAP 2

Elephant Range and Density

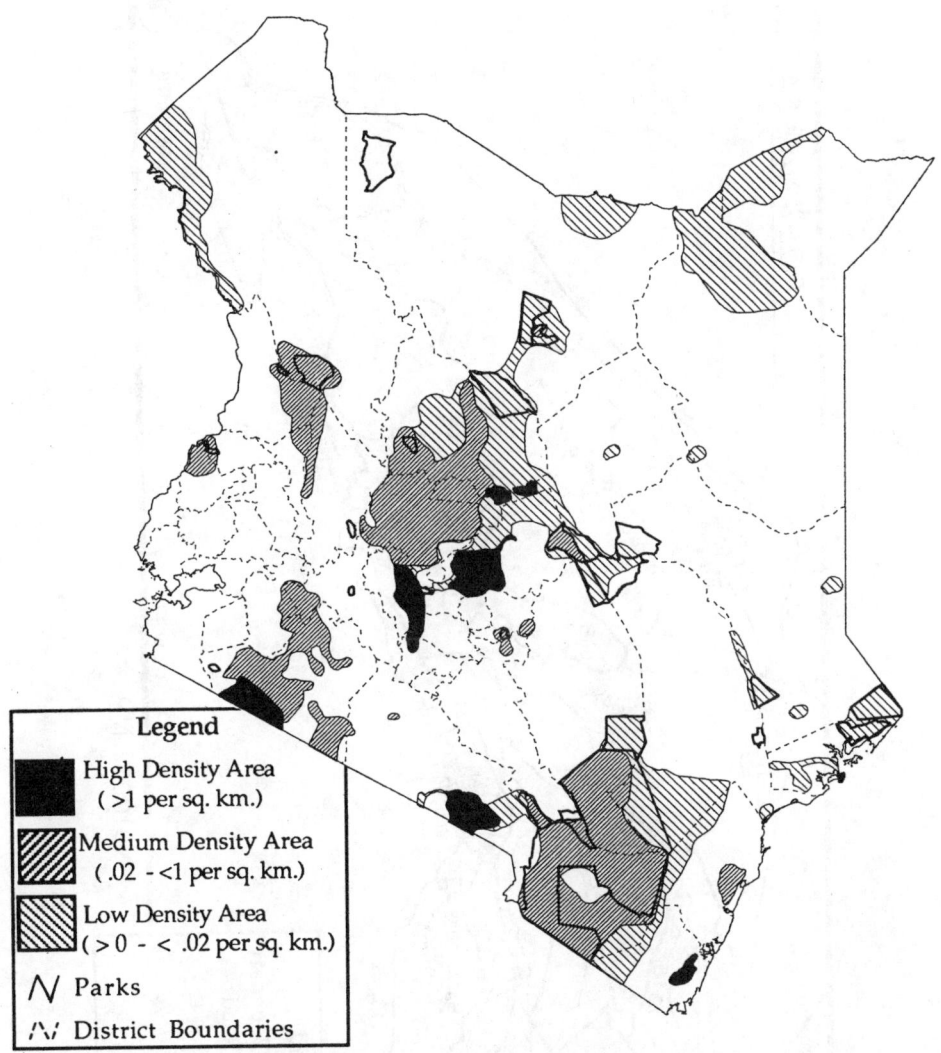

Legend

■ High Density Area
(>1 per sq. km.)

▨ Medium Density Area
(.02 - <1 per sq. km.)

▨ Low Density Area
(> 0 - < .02 per sq. km.)

∧ Parks

⋀ District Boundaries

Density distribution map of Kenya's elephant population in 1992
based on KWS aerial surveys, forest surveys and wardens' reports.

Prepared by: Ministry of Planning and National Development, Department of Resource Surveys
and Remote Servicing (DRSRS), and Kenya Wildlife Service (KWS).
Source of data: KWS, February, 1992

MAP 3

Nairobi National Park

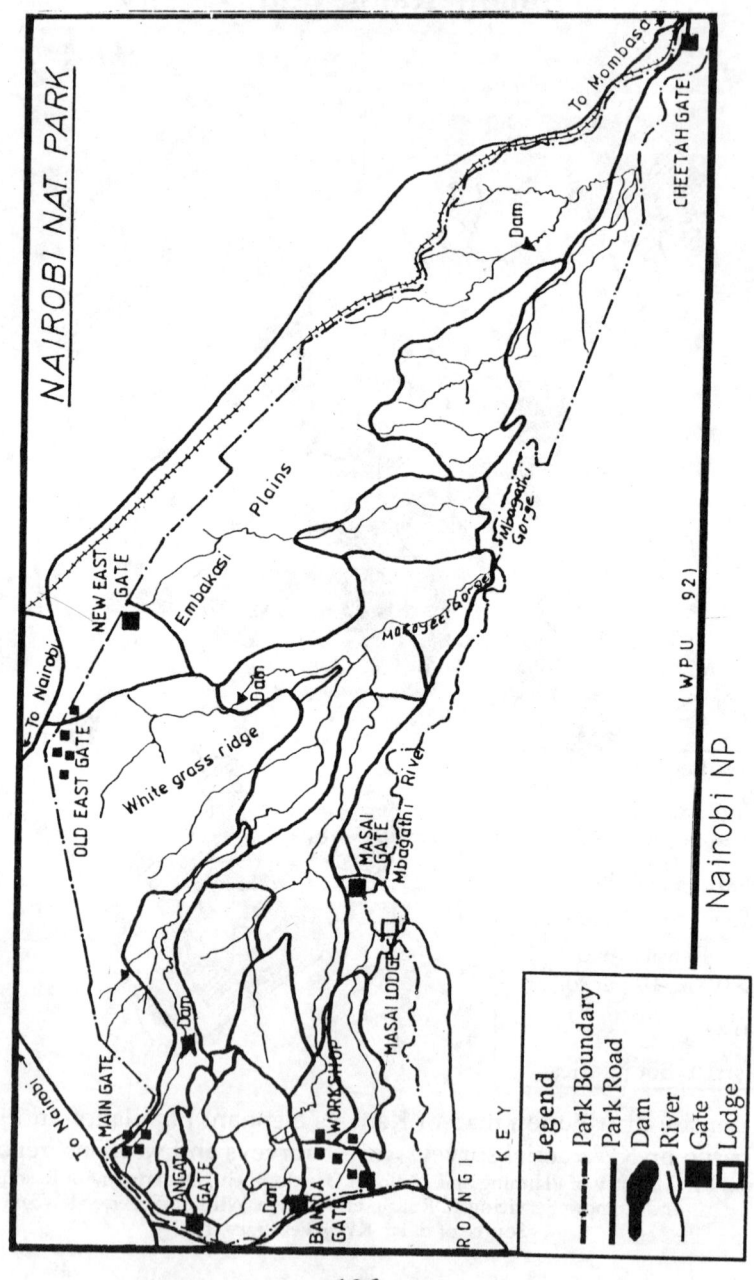

NAIROBI NAT. PARK

To Mombasa

CHEETAH GATE

Dam

Plains

Mbagathi Gorge

NEW EAST GATE

Embakasi

MOKOYEET GORGE

To Nairobi

OLD EAST GATE

Dam

White grass ridge

Mbagathi River

MASAI GATE

MASAI LODGE

Dam

To Nairobi

MAIN GATE

WORKSHOP

LANGATA GATE

BANDA GATE

Dam

R O N G I

(W P U 92)

Nairobi NP

Legend

KEY

_____ Park Boundary

_____ Park Road

Dam

River

■ Gate

□ Lodge

MAP 4

Mount Longonot National Park

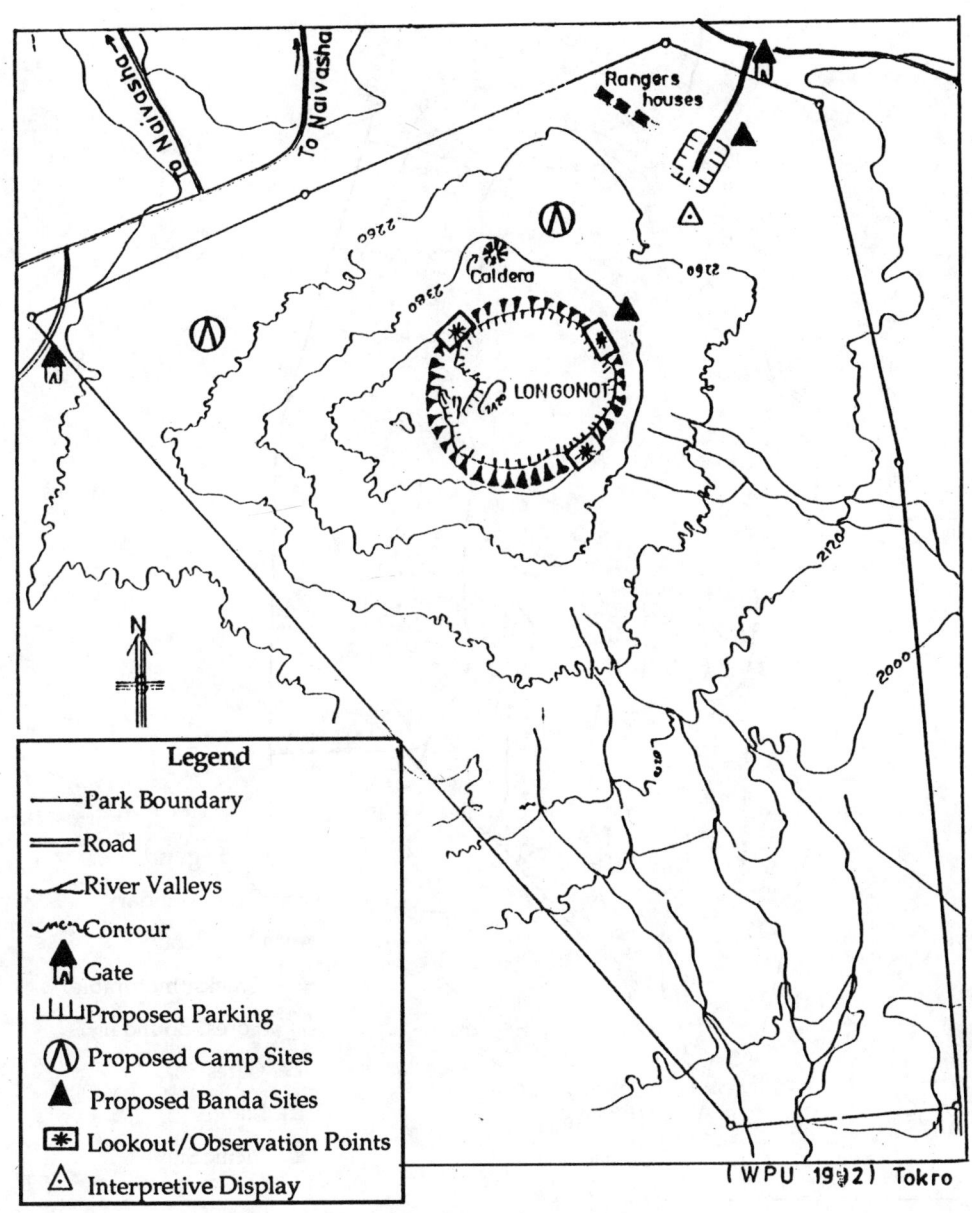

Rangers houses

Caldera

LONGONOT

To Naivasha

DUSDAIDN C.

N

Legend

—— Park Boundary

=== Road

River Valleys

Contour

Gate

Proposed Parking

Proposed Camp Sites

Proposed Banda Sites

Lookout/Observation Points

Interpretive Display

(WPU 1992) Tokro

MAP 5

Lake Nakuru National Park

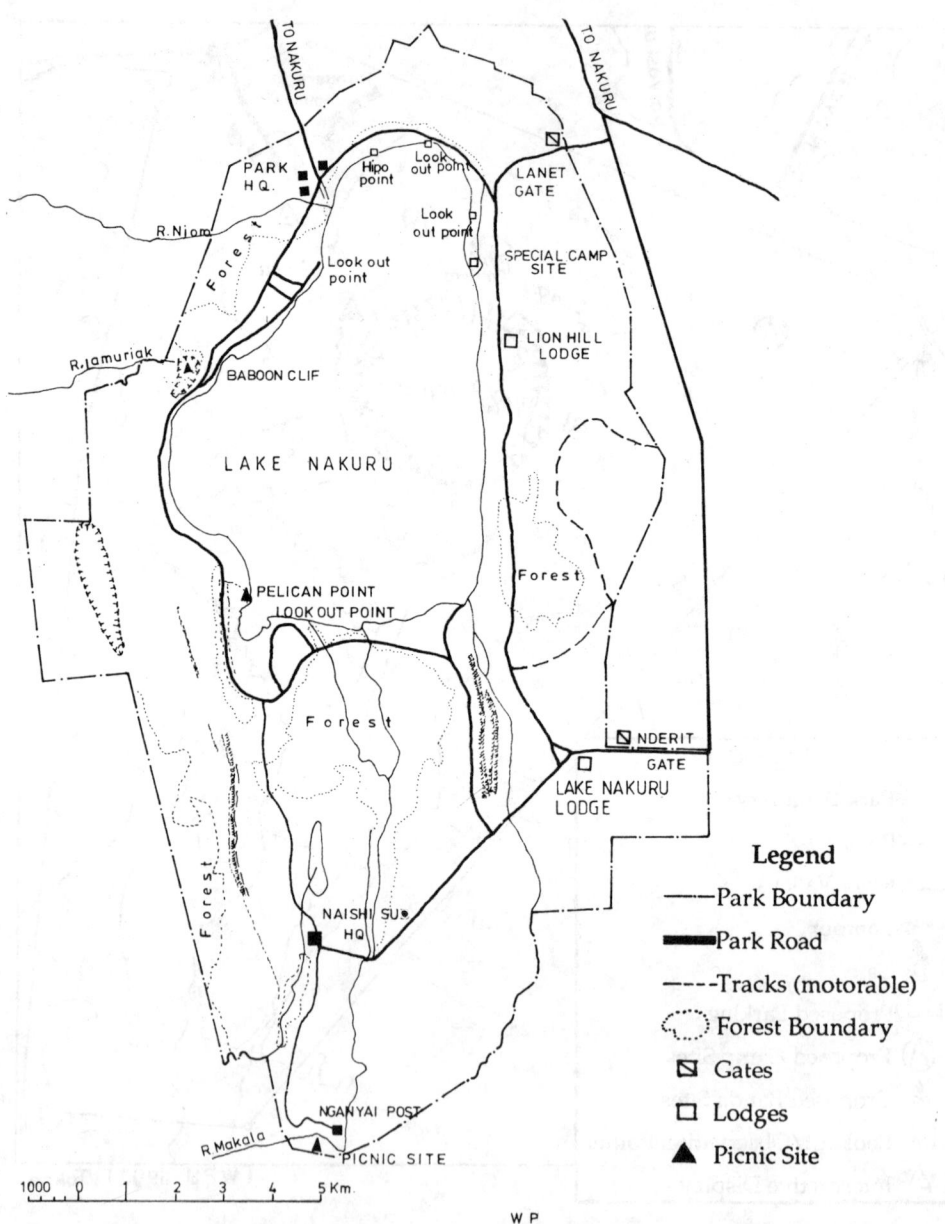

TO NAKURU

TO NAKURU

PARK
HQ.

Hipo
point

Look
out point

LANET
GATE

R. Njora

Forest

Look out
point

SPECIAL CAMP
SITE

Look out
point

LION HILL
LODGE

R. Iamuriak

BABOON CLIF

LAKE NAKURU

Forest

PELICAN POINT
LOOK OUT POINT

Forest

NDERIT

GATE

Forest

LAKE NAKURU
LODGE

NAISHI SU
HQ

NGANYAI POST

R. Makala

PICNIC SITE

Legend

—— Park Boundary

▬▬ Park Road

---- Tracks (motorable)

⟨⟩ Forest Boundary

◪ Gates

◻ Lodges

▲ Picnic Site

1000 0 1 2 3 4 5 Km.

W P.

MAP 6

Masai Mara National Reserve

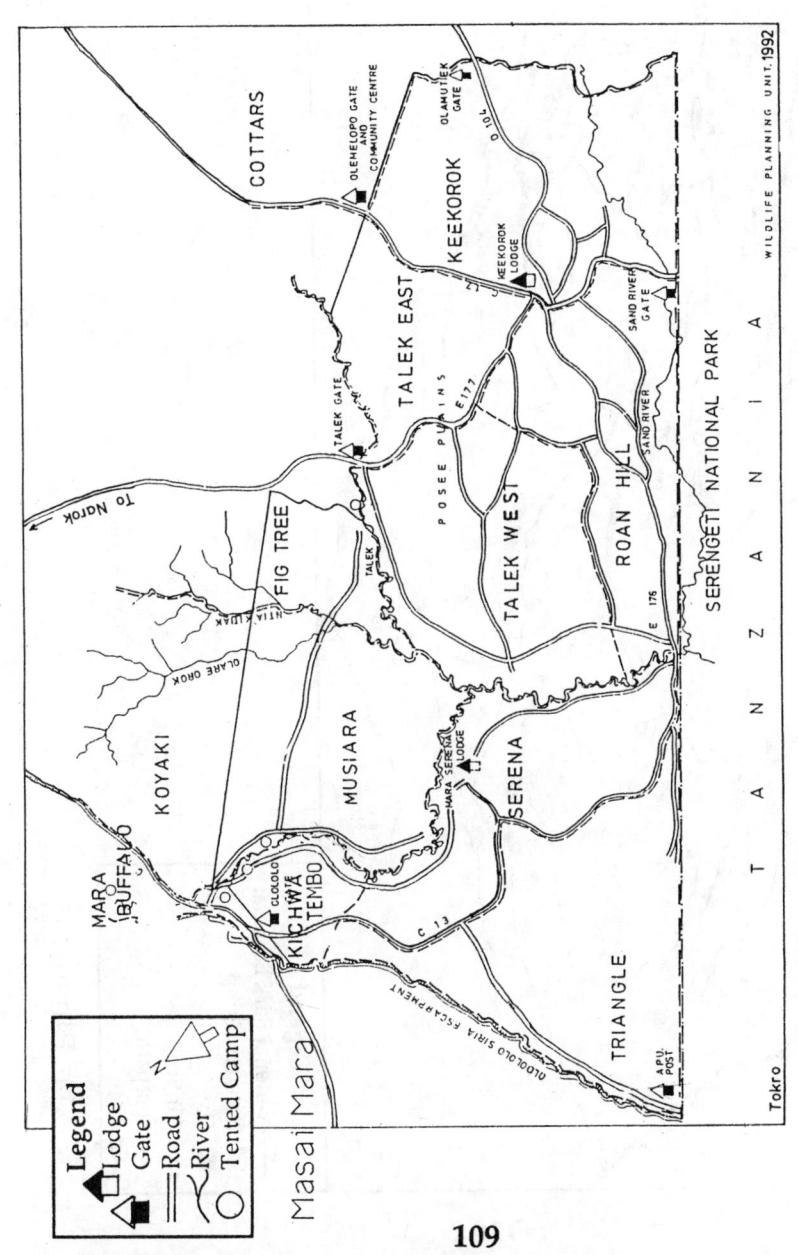

MAP 7

Mount Elgon National Park

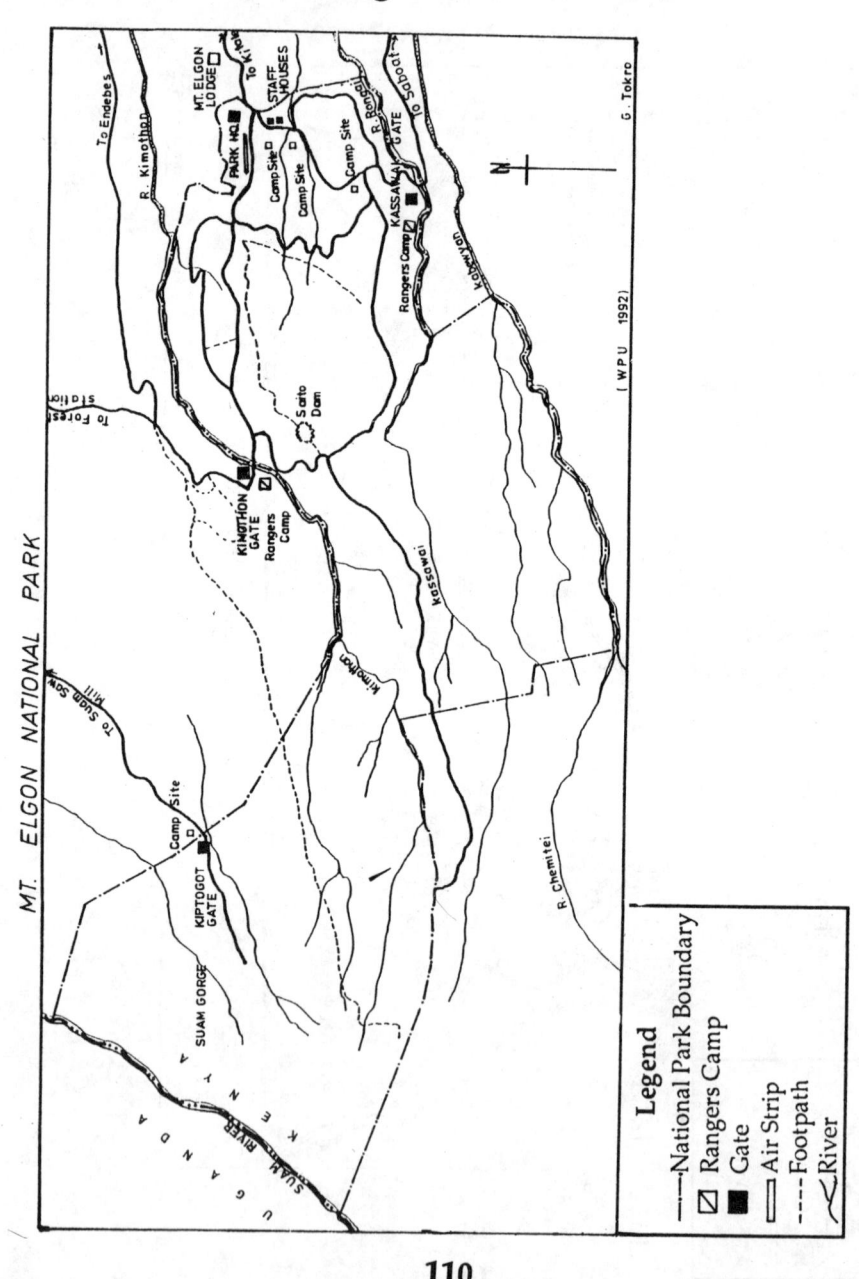

Mt Elgon

MAP 8

Ol Donyo Sabuk National Park

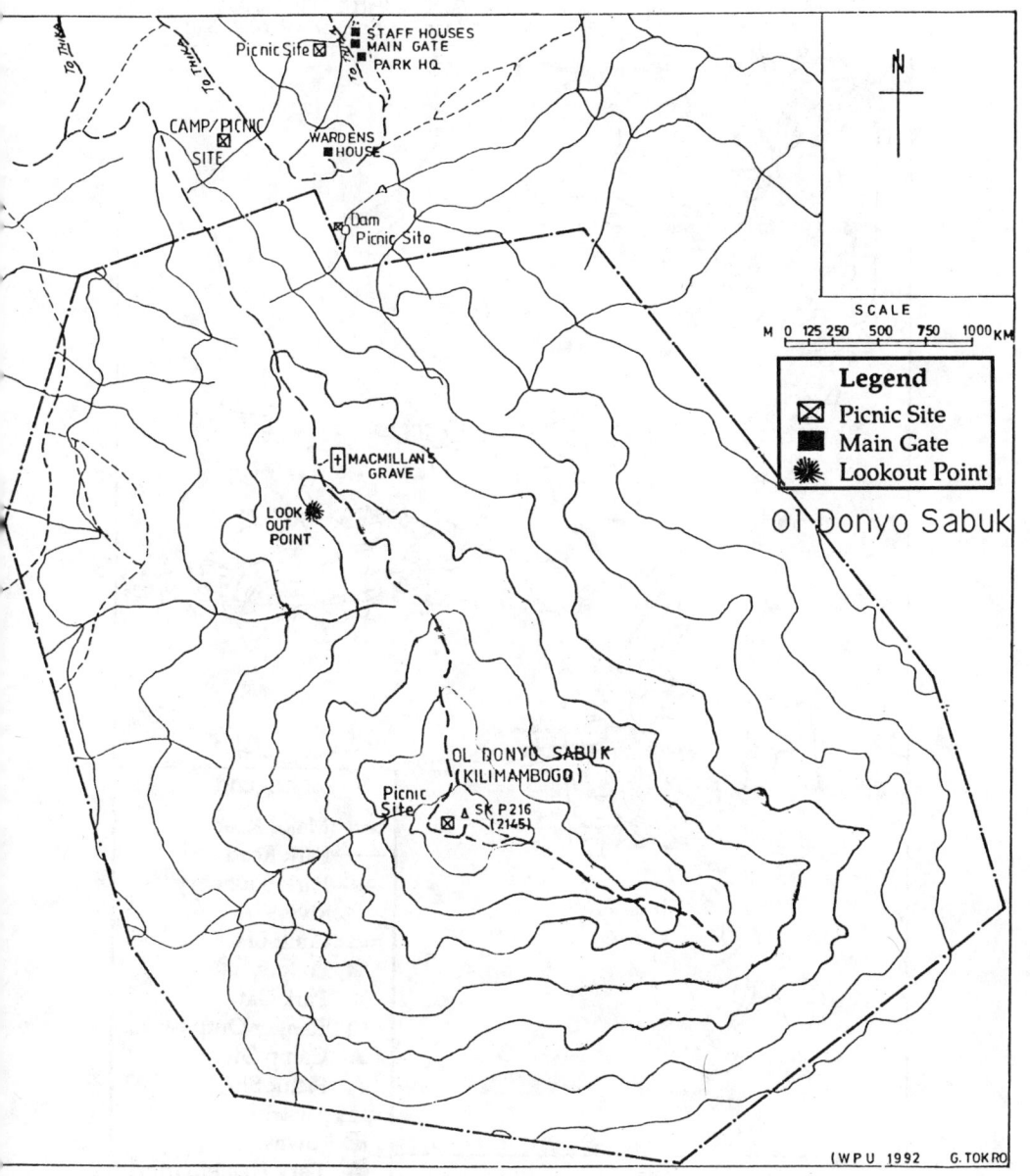

MAP 9

Aberdares National Park

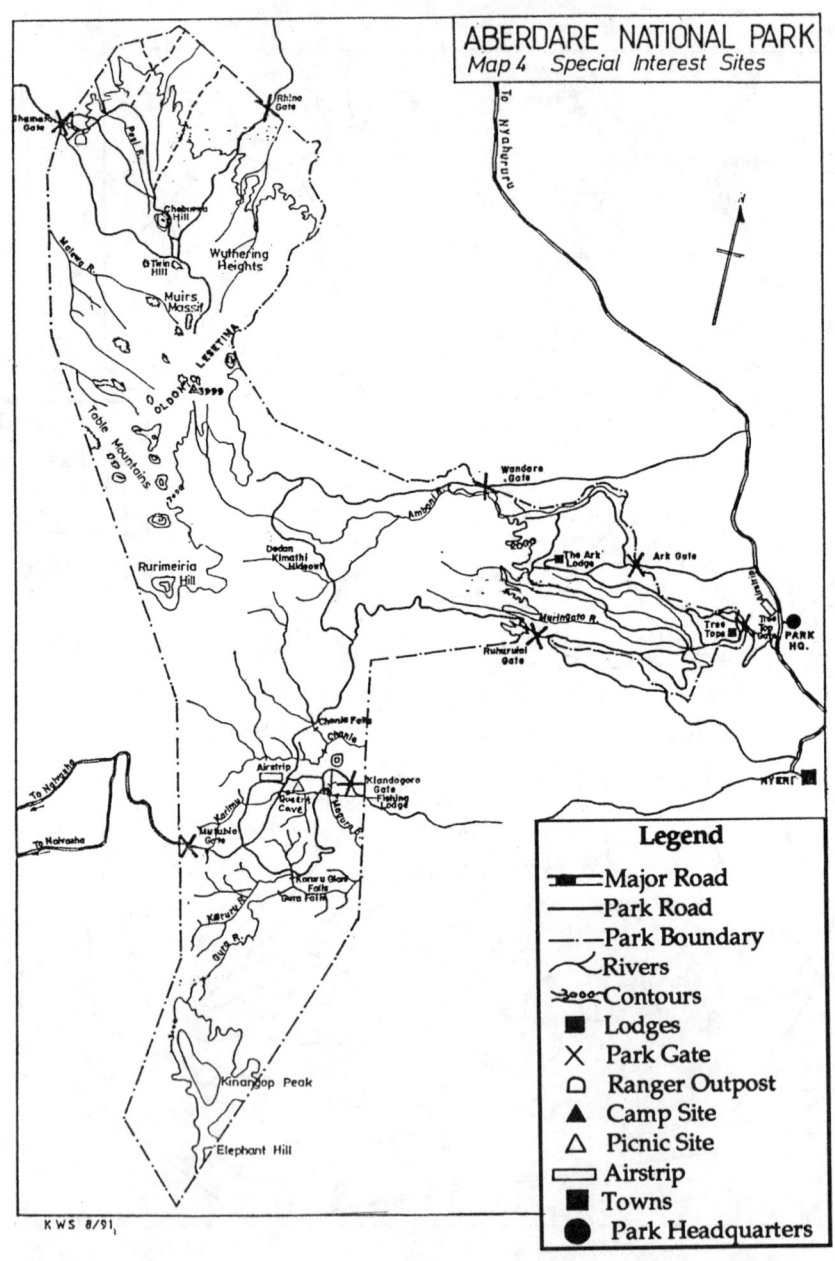

ABERDARE NATIONAL PARK
Map 4   Special Interest Sites

Legend

▬■▬	Major Road
—	Park Road
—·—	Park Boundary
⌇	Rivers
∿	Contours
■	Lodges
✕	Park Gate
⌂	Ranger Outpost
▲	Camp Site
△	Picnic Site
▭	Airstrip
■	Towns
●	Park Headquarters

KWS 8/91

MAP 10

Meru National Park

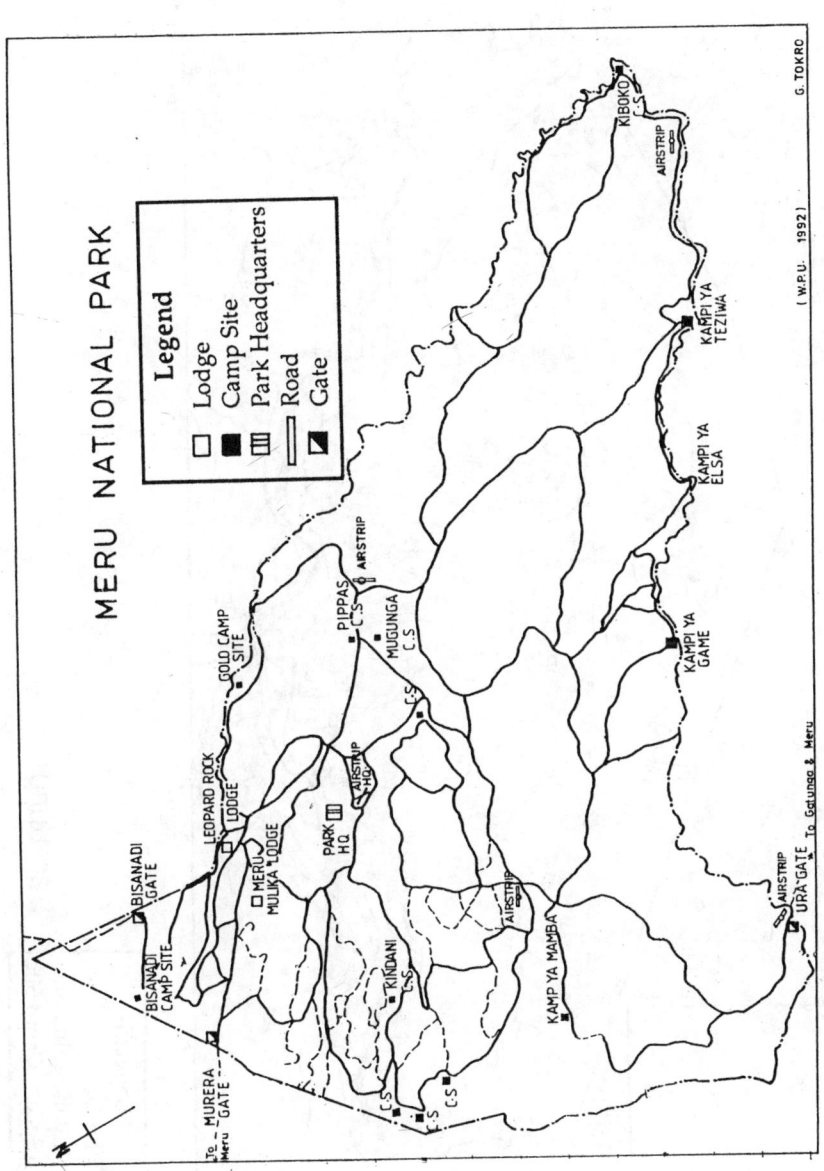

MAP 11

Samburu National Reserve

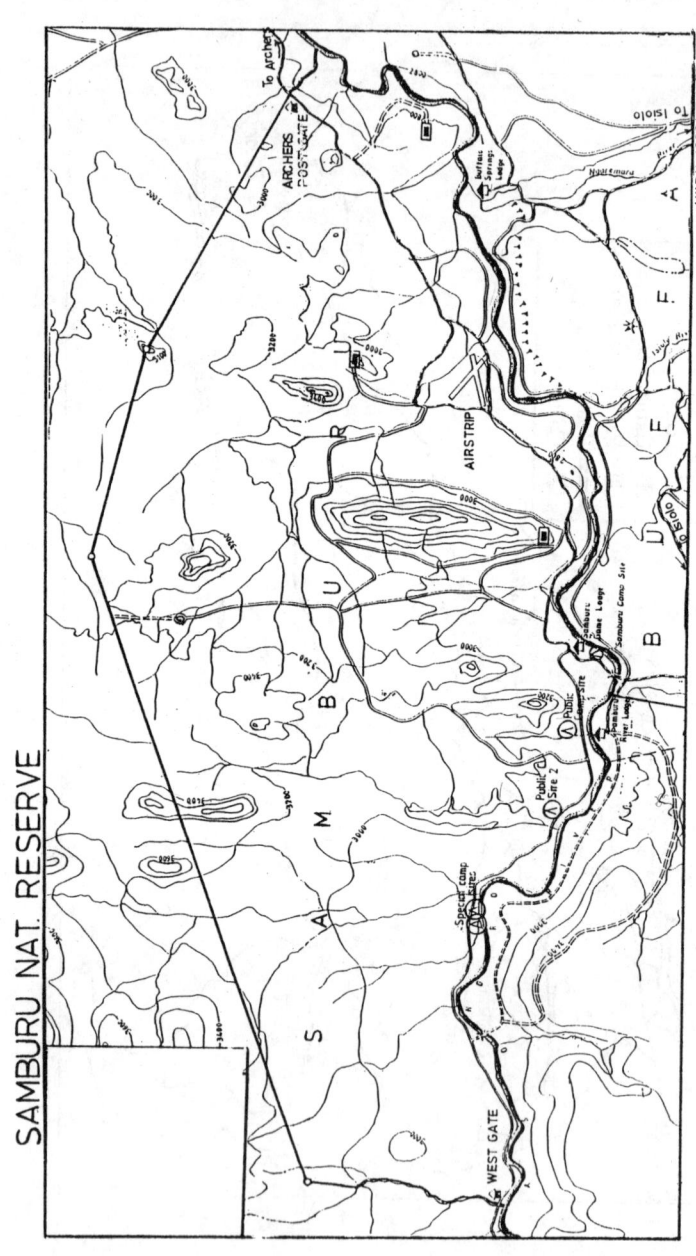

Legend

Lodge
Ⓚ Public Camp Site
Ⓐ Special Camp Site

Samburu

MAP 12

Buffalo Springs National Reserve

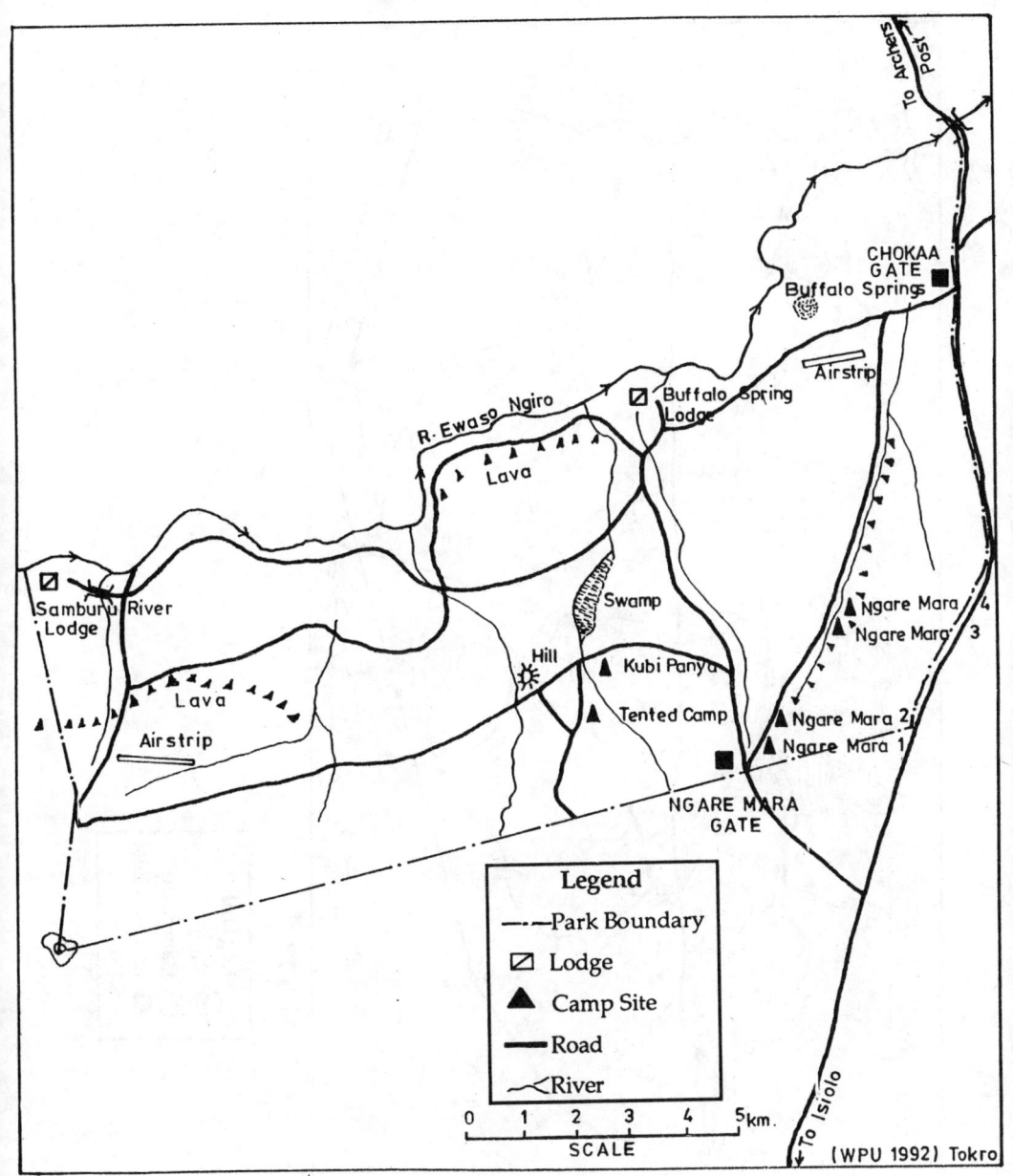

MAP 13

Shaba National Reserve

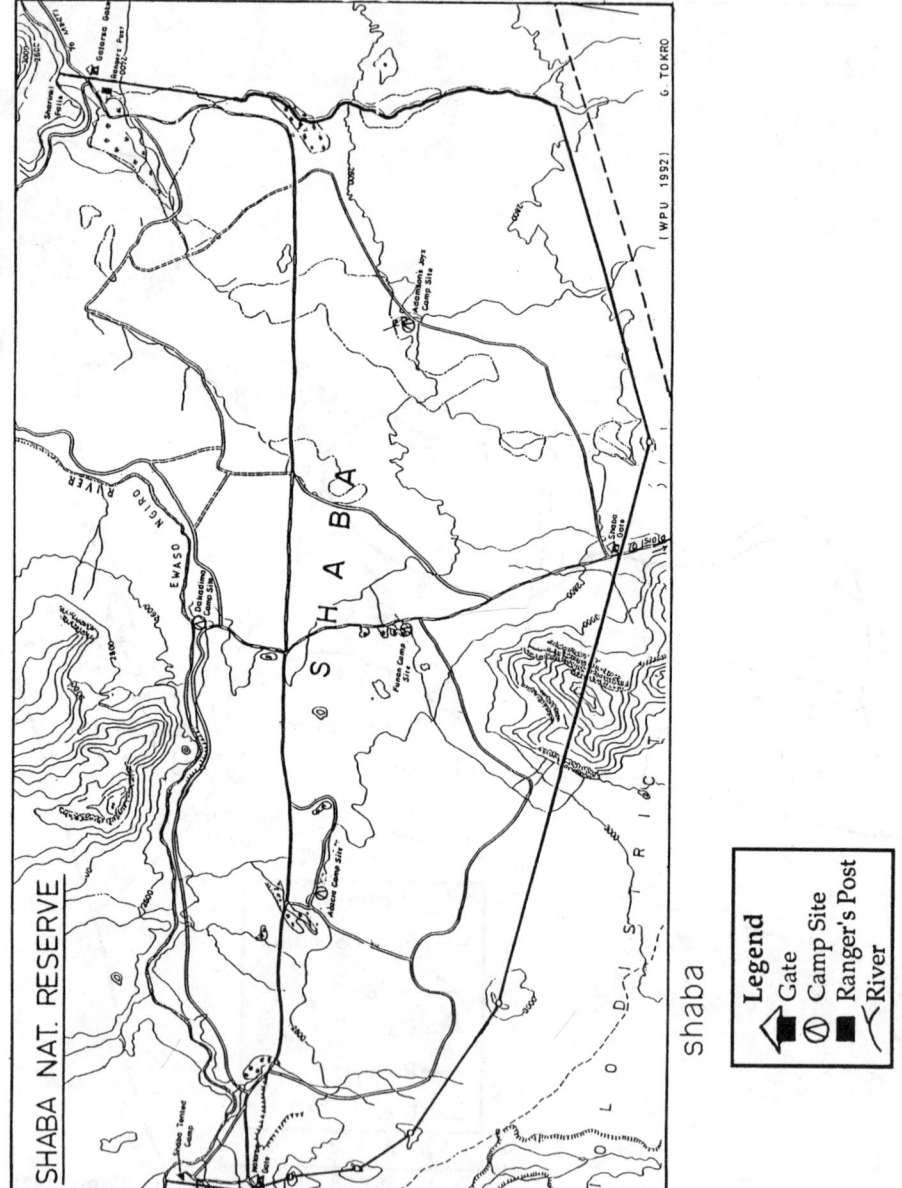

MAP 14

Marsabit National Park and Reserve

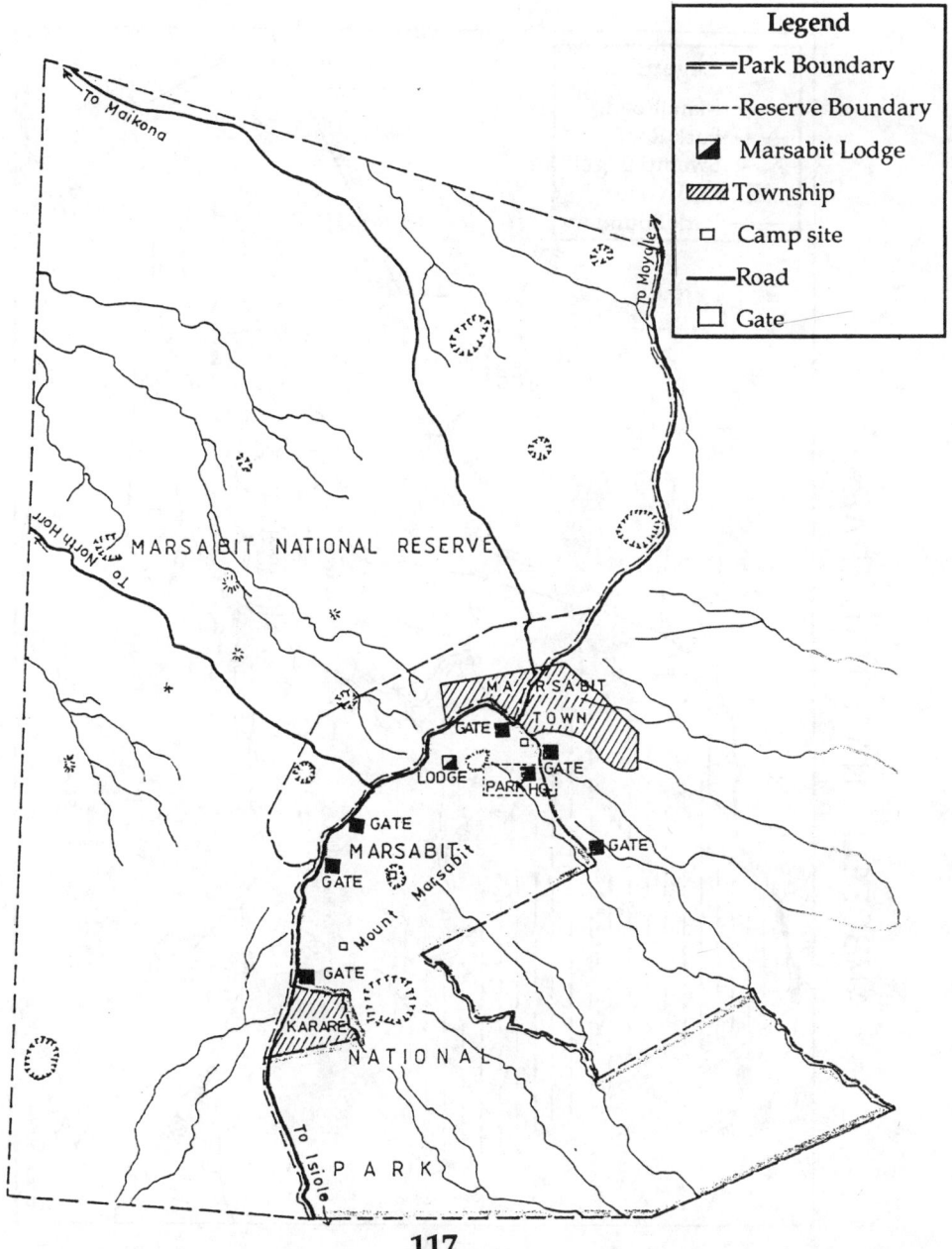

Legend
- ═══ Park Boundary
- --- Reserve Boundary
- ◪ Marsabit Lodge
- ▨ Township
- □ Camp site
- ── Road
- ☐ Gate

To Maikona

To Moyale

MARSABIT NATIONAL RESERVE

To North Horr

MA RSABIT TOWN

GATE

LODGE

PARK HQ

GATE

GATE

MARSABIT

GATE

GATE

Mount Marsabit

GATE

KARARE

NATIONAL

To Isiolo

PARK

MAP 15

Amboseli National Park

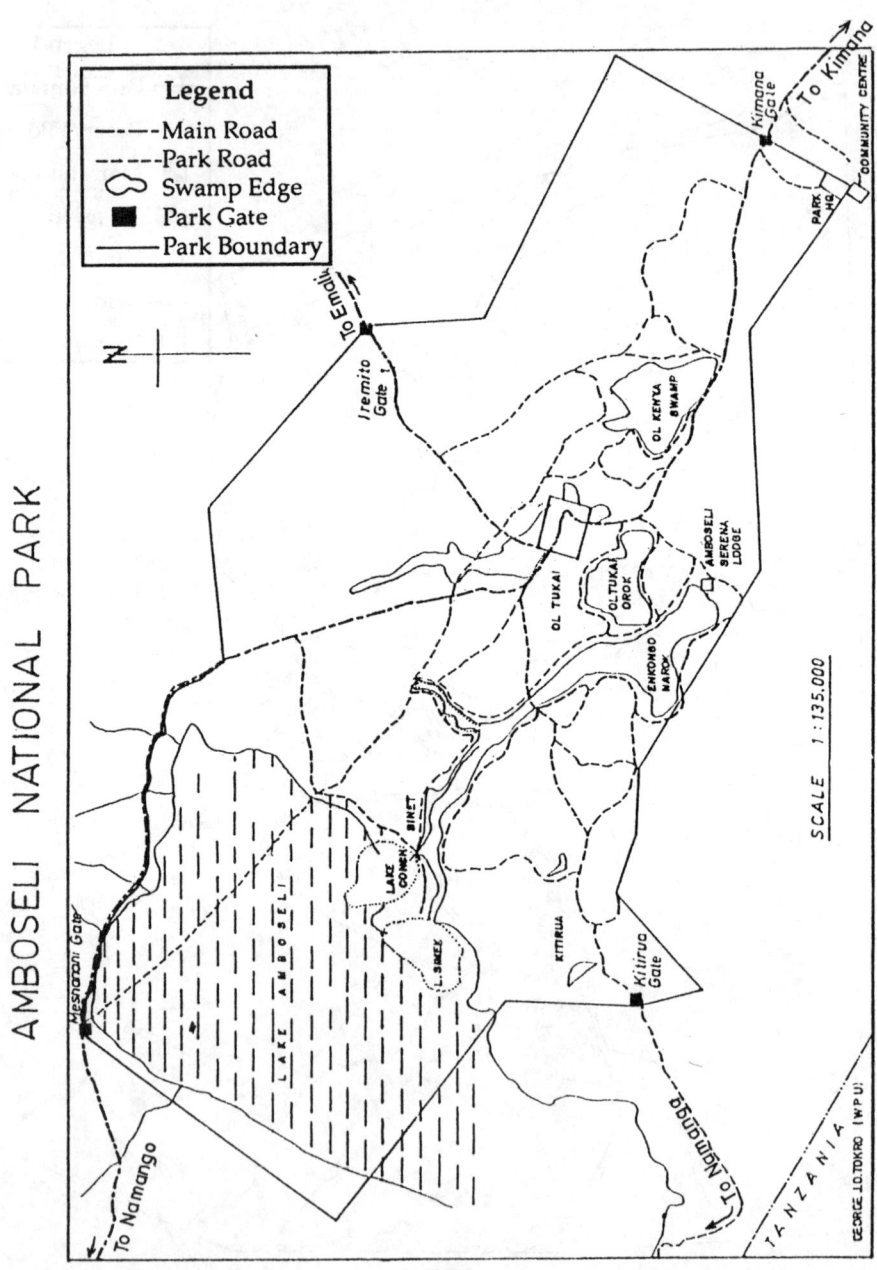

Legend
- - - Main Road
- - - Park Road
- Swamp Edge
- Park Gate
- Park Boundary

AMBOSELI NATIONAL PARK

SCALE 1:135.000

GEORGE LD.TOKPO (WPU)

MAP 16

Tsavo West National Park

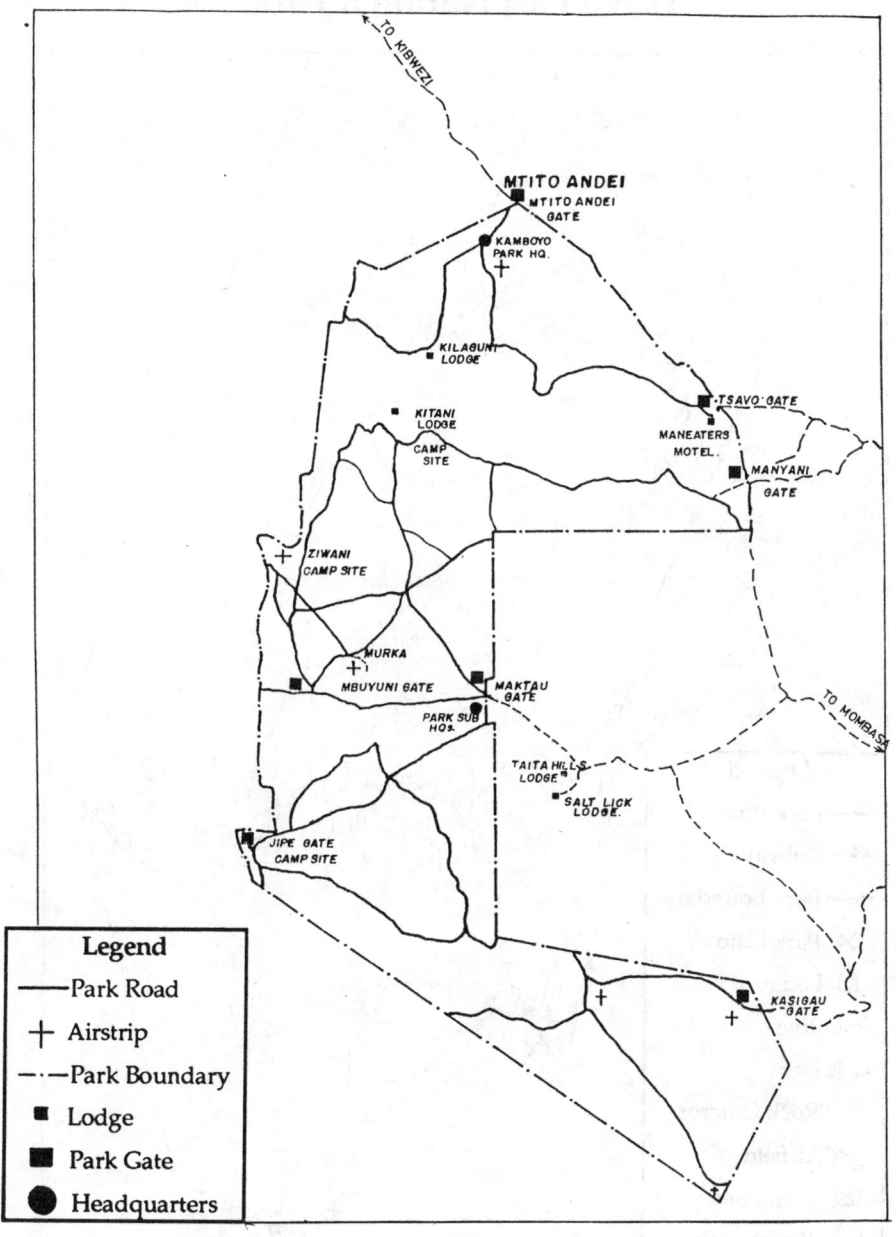

TO KIBWEZI

MTITO ANDEI
MTITO ANDEI
GATE

KAMBOYO
PARK HQ.

KILAGUNI
LODGE

KITANI
LODGE

TSAVO GATE

CAMP
SITE

MANEATERS
MOTEL.

MANYANI
GATE

ZIWANI
CAMP SITE

MURKA

MBUYUNI GATE

MAKTAU
GATE

PARK SUB
HQ.

TAITA HILLS
LODGE

TO MOMBASA

SALT LICK
LODGE.

JIPE GATE
CAMP SITE

Legend

—— Park Road

+ Airstrip

—·— Park Boundary

■ Lodge

▮ Park Gate

● Headquarters

KASIGAU
GATE

MAP 17

Tsavo East National Park

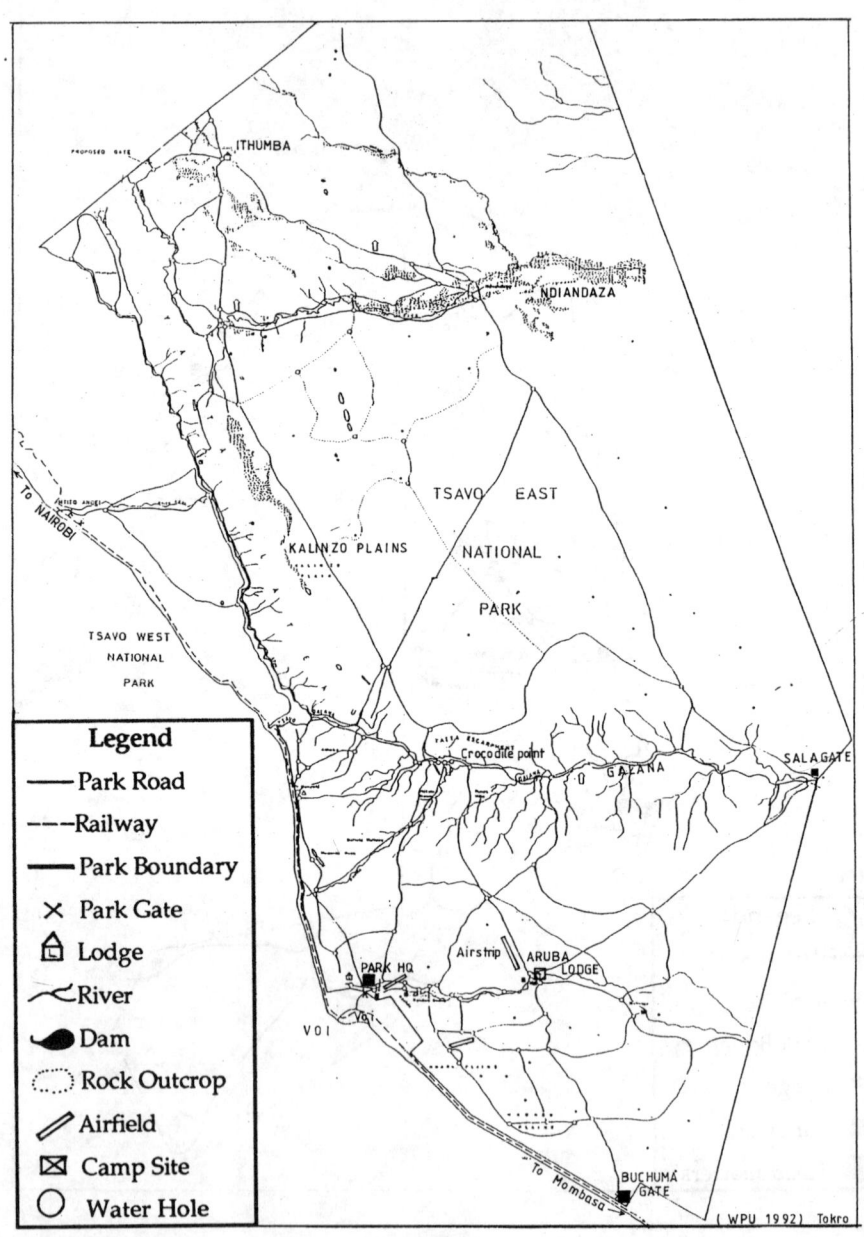

Legend

— Park Road

--- Railway

— Park Boundary

✕ Park Gate

⌂ Lodge

〰 River

🖤 Dam

⋯ Rock Outcrop

⟋ Airfield

⊠ Camp Site

○ Water Hole

ITHUMBA

NDIANDAZA

To NAIROBI

TSAVO EAST

KALINZO PLAINS

NATIONAL

PARK

TSAVO WEST
NATIONAL
PARK

Crocodile point

GALANA

SALA GATE

Airstrip

PARK HQ

ARUBA LODGE

VOI

BUCHUMA GATE

To Mombasa

(WPU 1992) Tokro

120

MAP 18

Shimba Hills National Reserve

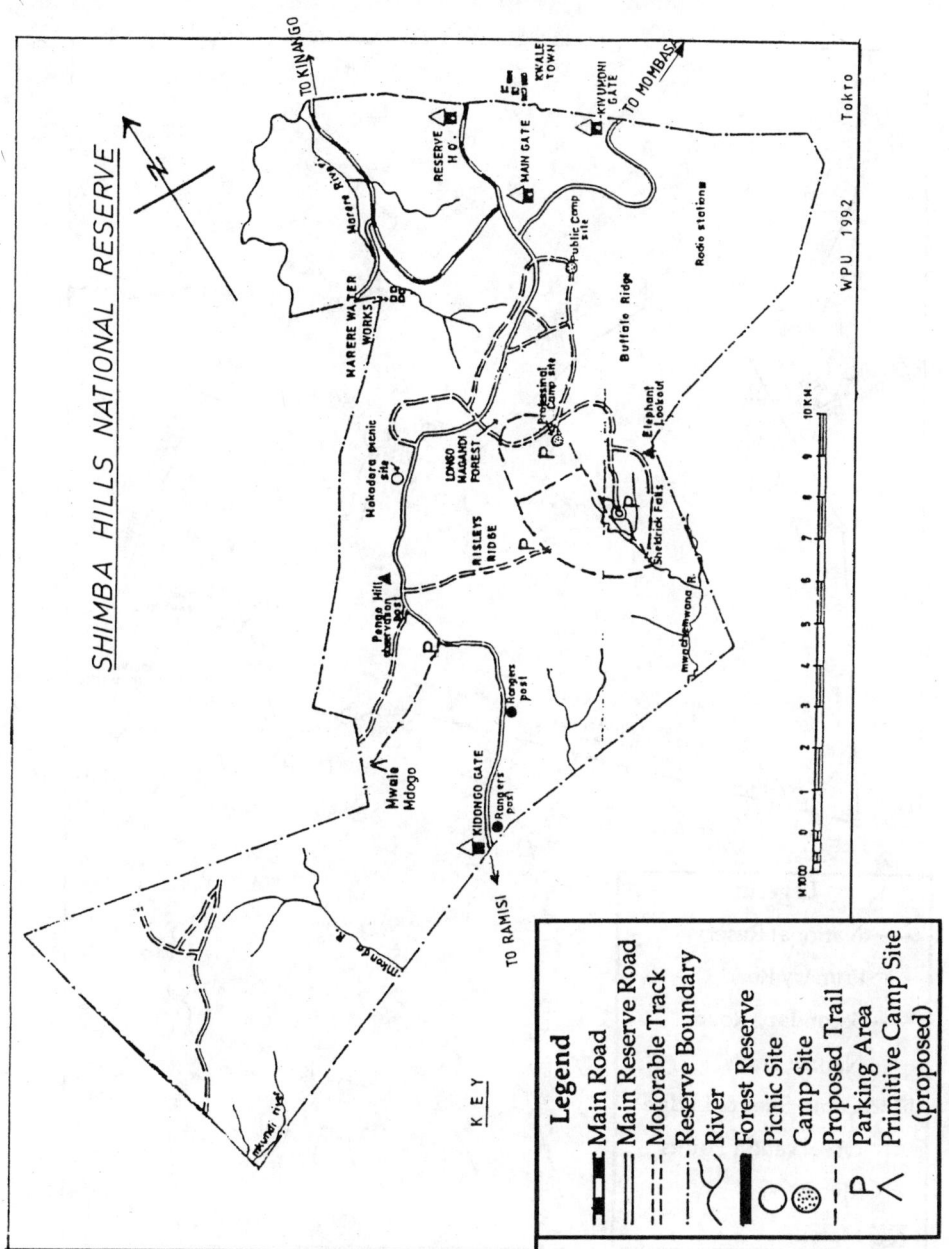

SHIMBA HILLS NATIONAL RESERVE

TO KINANGO

KWALE TOWN

TO MOMBASA

KITUVUONI GATE

RESERVE H.Q.

MAIN GATE

Mwereni River

Public Camp Site

MARERE WATER WORKS

Buffalo Ridge

Radio stations

Elephant Lookout

Professional Camp Site

Makadara picnic site

LONGO MAGANDI FOREST

Sheldrick Falls

RISLEYS RIDGE

mwachwawongo R.

Pengo Hills observation post

Rangers post

Mwele Mdogo

KIDONGO GATE

Rangers post

TO RAMISI

Mkurumdzi R.

Mwaluganje R.

WPU 1992   Tokro

10 KM.

KM000 0 1 2 3 4 5 6 7 8 9 10 KM.

Legend

K E Y

- Main Road
- Main Reserve Road
- Motorable Track
- Reserve Boundary
- River
- Forest Reserve
- ◯ Picnic Site
- ⊚ Camp Site
- Proposed Trail
- P Parking Area
- ⋀ Primitive Camp Site (proposed)

MAP 19

Laikipia National Reserve

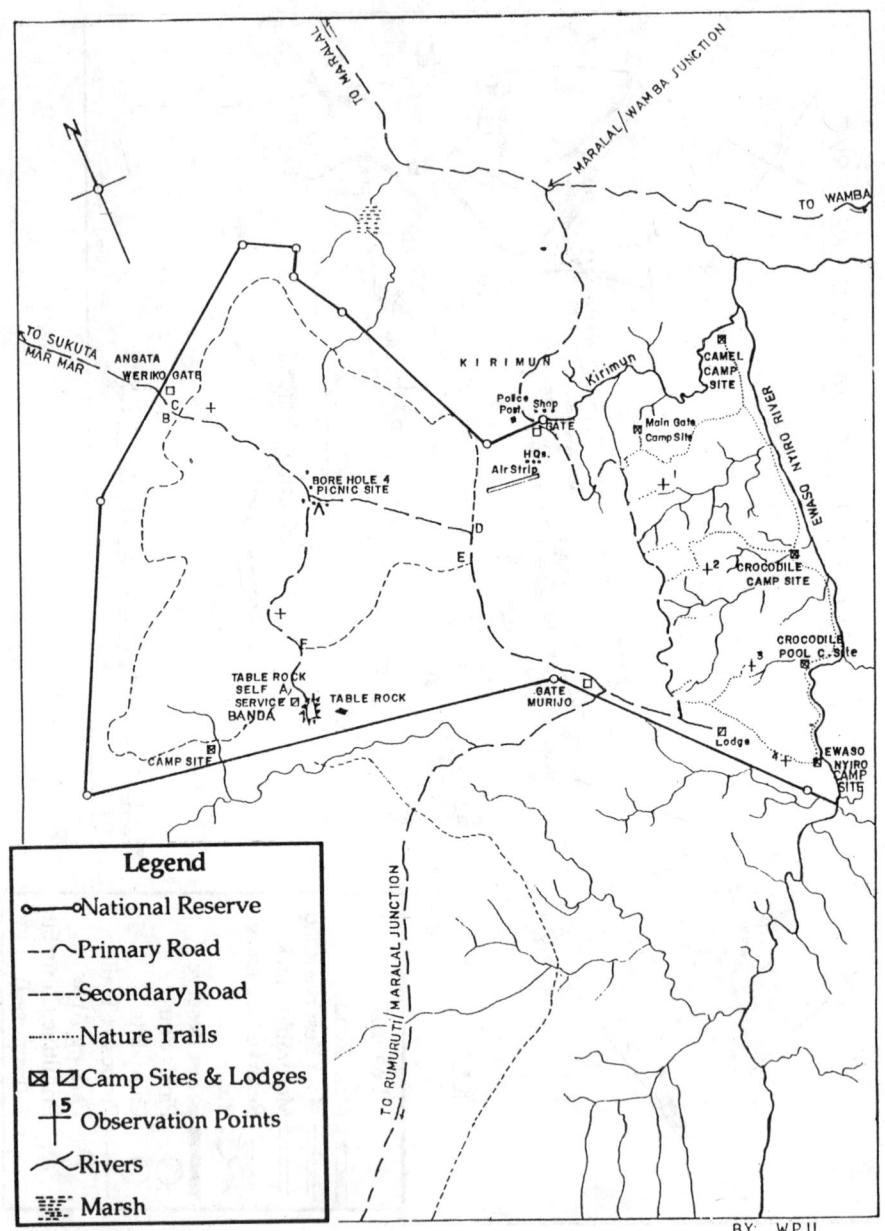

Legend

- ○—○ National Reserve
- --⌒ Primary Road
- ----- Secondary Road
- ········· Nature Trails
- ⊠ ⬚ Camp Sites & Lodges
- ┼⁵ Observation Points
- ⌒ Rivers
- ☷ Marsh

BY: W.P.U

Wildlife
Chart

Wildlife Chart

NATIONAL PARKS

NATIONAL PARKS	Aardvark	Antelope Roan	Sable	Baboon Olive	Yellow	Bongo	Buffalo	Bushbuck	Cheetah	Crocodile	Dikdik Guenther's	Kirk's	Duiker Common
Aberdares				•		•	•	•					•
Amboseli					•		•	•	•			•	•
Hells Gate/Longonot				•			•	•	•			•	•
Kora				•			•	•	•	•		•	•
Lake Nakuru				•			•	•	•			•	•
Meru	•			•			•	•	•			•	•
Mount Elgon	•			•			•	•					•
Mount Kenya				•		•	•	•					•
Nairobi	•			•			•	•	•	•		•	•
Ol Donyo Sabuk	•			•			•	•	•			•	•
Ruma	•	•			•		•	•				•	•
Saiwa Swamp	•			•				•				•	•
Sibiloi	•			•					•	•		•	
South Island	•			•								•	•
Tsavo East	•				•		•	•	•	•		•	•
Tsavo West	•				•		•	•	•	•		•	•

NATIONAL RESERVES

NATIONAL RESERVES	Aardvark	Antelope Roan	Sable	Baboon Olive	Yellow	Bongo	Buffalo	Bushbuck	Cheetah	Crocodile	Dikdik Guenther's	Kirk's	Duiker Common
Arawale	•			•			•	•	•			•	•
Bisanadi/Meru	•			•			•	•	•	•		•	•
Buffalo Springs	•			•			•	•	•	•	•	•	•
Kakamega	•			•			•	•				•	•
Kamnarok	•			•			•	•	•			•	•
Lake Bogoria	•			•			•		•		•	•	•
Marsabit	•			•			•	•	•		•	•	•
Masai Mara	•	•		•			•	•	•	•		•	•
Mwea				•			•	•	•			•	•
Nasolot				•			•	•			•	•	•
Samburu	•			•			•	•	•	•	•	•	•
Shaba	•			•			•	•	•	•		•	•
Shimba Hills	•	•	•	•			•	•				•	•
Tana River Primate				•						•		•	•

124

Duiker Red	Blue	Black fronted	Yellow backed	Eland	Elephant	Gazelle Grant's	Thomson's	Gerenuk	Giant Forest Hog	Giraffe Masai	Reticulated	Rothschild	Hartebeest Cok'e	Hunter's	Jackson's	Hippopotamus	Hunting Dog	Hyena Striped
	•			•	•				•								•	
•				•	•	•	•	•		•			•			•	•	•
				•	•	•	•			•			•			•		•
				•	•	•	•	•			•		•			•	•	
				•		•	•					•				•		•
	•			•	•	•	•				•		•			•	•	•
•	•	•		•	•				•							•	•	
•	•	•		•	•				•								•	
				•		•	•			•			•			•	•	•
					•											•	•	
												•			•	•		
•	•								•									
				•		•				•						•	•	•
				•		•										•		
•	•			•	•	•	•			•			•	•		•	•	•
•	•			•	•	•	•	•		•			•			•	•	•

Duiker Red	Blue	Black fronted	Yellow backed	Eland	Elephant	Gazelle Grant's	Thomson's	Gerenuk	Giant Forest Hog	Giraffe Masai	Reticulated	Rothschild	Hartebeest Cok'e	Hunter's	Jackson's	Hippopotamus	Hunting Dog	Hyena Striped
				•	•	•								•		•		
				•	•	•		•		•			•			•	•	
•	•			•	•	•		•		•						•	•	•
			•	•		•												
				•	•	•												
						•		•					•					•
				•	•	•		•			•							•
•	•			•	•	•	•		•	•			•			•	•	•
				•	•	•										•		
				•		•						•				•		
•	•			•	•	•		•		•						•	•	•
				•	•	•		•		•						•	•	•
•	•					•			•									
•				•	•	•				•	•					•	•	

125

Wildlife Chart continued

NATIONAL PARKS

	Hyena Spotted	Impala	Klipspringer	Kudu Greater	Lesser	Leopard	Lion	Monkey De Brazza	B & W colobus	Red colobus	Mangabey	Patas	Sykes/Blue
Aberdares	•	•	•			•	•		•				•
Amboseli	•	•	•		•	•	•						•
Hells Gate/Longonot	•	•	•			•	•						•
Kora	•	•			•	•	•						•
Lake Nakuru	•	•	•			•	•		•				•
Meru	•	•			•	•	•		•			•	•
Mount Elgon	•		•			•	•	•	•				•
Mount Kenya	•		•			•	•		•				•
Nairobi	•	•	•			•	•						•
Ol Donyo Sabuk	•	•				•							
Ruma	•	•				•							
Saiwa Swamp								•	•				•
Sibiloi		•		•	•	•	•						
South Island		•											•
Tsavo East	•	•	•		•	•	•						•
Tsavo West	•	•	•		•	•	•						•

NATIONAL RESERVES

	Hyena Spotted	Impala	Klipspringer	Kudu Greater	Lesser	Leopard	Lion	Monkey De Brazza	B & W colobus	Red colobus	Mangabey	Patas	Sykes/Blue
Arawale		•				•	•						•
Bisanadi/Meru		•				•	•						•
Buffalo Springs	•	•	•		•	•	•						•
Kakamega		•				•	•	•					•
Kamnarok		•					•						•
Lake Bogoria	•	•	•	•		•							
Marsabit	•	•	•	•	•	•	•					•	•
Masai Mara	•	•	•			•	•		•			•	•
Mwea		•				•	•						•
Nasolot		•				•	•						•
Samburu	•	•	•		•	•	•						•
Shaba	•	•	•		•	•	•						•
Shimba Hills						•	•			•			•
Tana River Primate		•			•	•	•	•	•	•	•		•

Monkey Red tailed	Oryx Beisa	Fringe-eared	Potto	Reedbuck Bohor	Chanler's	Rhinoceros Black	White	Serval Cat	Sitatunga	Suni	Topi	Waterbuck Common	Defassa	Wildebeest	Zebra Burchell's	Grevy	Other	Other
				•	•	•		•		•		•						
		•		•		•		•				•		•	•			
		•		•	•			•				•			•			
	•			•				•				•			•			
				•	•	•	•	•										
	•			•				•		•		•			•	•		
				•	•			•		•					•			
				•	•	•		•		•			•		•			
				•	•	•		•				•	•	•	•			
				•											•			
				•				•			•	•						
									•			•						
	•		•									•			•	•		
															•			
		•		•		•		•		•		•			•	•		
		•		•		•		•		•		•		•	•			

Monkey Red tailed	Oryx Beisa	Fringe-eared	Potto	Reedbuck Bohor	Chanler's	Rhinoceros Black	White	Serval Cat	Sitatunga	Suni	Topi	Waterbuck Common	Defassa	Wildebeest	Zebra Burchell's	Grevy	Other	Other
				•							•				•			
				•				•							•			
	•			•				•				•			•	•		
•				•											•			
				•											•			
				•	•										•			
	•							•							•	•		
•				•	•	•		•		•	•		•	•	•			
				•											•			
				•											•			
	•							•				•			•	•		
	•			•				•				•			•	•		
				•				•				•			•			
	•	•										•			•	•		

Glossary of Terms Used

algae a type of plant with no stems or leaves which grows on damp surfaces and are green and slimy.

alkali a substance or liquid which forms a chemical salt if it is combined with an acid.

amphibian an animal such as a frog that is able to live on land and in water.

aquatic an animal or plant that lives or grows in water.

bacteria are very small organisms which live in air, water, soil, plants and animals. Some bacteria can cause disease.

browser an animal that feed on twigs or leaves of plants.

caldera large volcanic crater made when the underground lava reservoirs collapsed

camouflage the way in which animals avoid being seen by blending in with their natural surroundings (through skin colouring, patterning, etc.)

carnivore an animal that mainly eats meat.

carrion the rotting flesh of dead animals.

commiphora belonging to a large family of trees and shrubs, often with resinous bark. Found in dry bushland below 1,700m (5,600ft)

crevice a narrow crack in rock or between large stones

ecology the pattern and balance of relation-ships between plants, animals, people and their environment in a particular region.

128

ecosystem	all the plants and animals that live in a particular area together with the complex relationship that exists between all of them and their environment.
effluent	liquid waste material that comes out of factories or sewage works.
euphorbia	a very large family of herbs, shrubs and trees, centred in the tropics and varying from tiny desert succulents to tall forest trees.
exotic	something strange, unusual and interesting because it comes from a distant country.
extinct	a species of animal or plant which no longer has any living members; no longer active (volcano).
fauna	animals.
flora	plants.
forage	search for food; forage crops are grown for livestock.
fumarole	a vent or opening in the surface of the earth.
fungus (pl. **fungi**)	a plant that has no flowers, leaves or green colouring. Mushrooms and toadstools are fungi. Other types of fungus such as mould and mildew are extremely small, spread quickly over surfaces, and look like a fine powder.
geyser	a hole in the earth's surface from which hot water and steam come out forcefully, usually at irregular intervals of time.
glacier	a huge mass of ice which moves very slowly, often down a mountain valley.
gorge	a deep, narrow valley with very steep sides, usually where a river passes through mountains or an area of hard rock.
grazer	an animal which eats grass or other plants.
gregarious	animals or birds normally living in large groups

giant groundsell   see senecio.

gully (pl.ies) a long narrow valley with steep sides.

hagenia   a tree which grows to a height of about 15m (50ft). Its bark is dark red-brown and flakes off irregularly; leaves reddish when young and flowers hang down.

herbivore   an animal that only eats plants.

hypericum a sub genus of a family of tropical trees and shrubs with eleven species occuring in East Africa.

immune   unaffected by something; able to escape something.

indigenous originally from the country in which it is found.

lateritic   residual clay formed under tropical climate conditions by weathering of igneous rocks.

lava   a kind of rock which comes out of a volcano in the form of a very hot liquid and gradually cools and becomes solid.

lichen   a cluster of tiny plants that looks like moss and grows on rocks, trees, walls, etc.

mammal   an animal, the female of which gives birth to babies not eggs and feeds them with milk from her body.

migratory   animals or birds that move at a particular time or season from one part of the world or of a country to another, usually in order to breed or to find new feeding grounds.

montane   forest found around mountains.

nomadic   a society or group of people that travel from place to place rather than living in one place all the time.

organic   something that is produced by or found in plants or animals.

pastoral   a way of life in which people live in the country and farm the land, especially by keeping animals that feed on the grass.

petrified   when something dies it gradually changes into stone.

plankton   a layer of tiny animals and plants that live in the surface layer of the sea.

predator   an animal that kills and eats other animals.

prey   the creatures that are hunted and eaten by an animal or bird in order to live; also used of wild animals that a human tries to catch and kill.

primate   one of the group of mammals which is the most intelligent and highly developed and which includes humans, monkeys, and apes.

propagate   to grow or increase in number.

radiation   energy, especially heat, that comes from a particular source, for example the sun.

reptile   a cold-blooded animal which has a scaly skin and lays eggs (tortoises, snakes, lizards and crocodiles are all reptiles.)

sanctuary   a place of safety for someone or something which is being hunted or chased.

savannah   an open, flat stretch of grassland.

scavenge   to get food by searching for and eating the meat of dead creatures and other waste food.

scree   a mass of loose stones on the side of a mountain.

scrub   low trees and bushes growing in an area that has very little rain.

sedentary   people or animals that are settled and do not travel from place to place.

senecio   71 species of senecio grow in East Africa. Tree senecios or giant groundsels are either trees or shrubs growing up to 9m (30ft) in height. There are only three species of this group in Kenya.

sewage   waste matter that has been used in homes and factories which is carried away in sewers.

swamp   an area of very wet land with wild plants growing in it.

terrestrial   living on land or on the ground rather than in the sea, in trees, or in the air.

territorial   concerned with the ownership of a particular area of land or water.

thicket   a small group of trees or bushes which are growing closely together.

translocate   to move from one place to another.

ultraviolet   ultraviolet light or radiation is what causes your skin to become darker in colour after you have been in sunlight. In large amounts ultraviolet light is harmful.

venomous   a snake, scorpion or spider which has a gland that produces poison which it uses to attack its enemy or prey.

References

CHAPTER 1   **The Beginnings of Conservation**

"First World Conference on National Parks ", IUCN,
    Seattle, Washington, USA, 1962 - Appendix C

CHAPTER 2   **Natural Resources Conservation**

"The Changing Atmosphere",
    UNEP, Environment Brief No. 1

"Action on Ozone" UNEP Report

CHAPTER 3   **The Significance of Wildlife
    and its Role in the Ecosystem**

"National State of the Environment Report"
    Kenya (2) 1987

"Soil Organisms"
    The New Encyclopaedia Britannica, Vol. 16

CHAPTER 4   **Common Wild Animal Communities and their Habitats**

"East Africa: The Advantages of Farming Game"
    by David Hopcraft, Span 13,1, 1970.

Judith Rudnai, Conservationist

CHAPTER 5   **Wildlife Conservation and Management**

"Wildlife Conservation and Management Act", Cap. 376,
    Laws of Kenya

National Parks - A World Need, Victor H. Cahalane

Conservation for Survival - An Ecological Strategy,
    Kai Curry Lindahl

Rhino Help International, Nairobi Office

Kenya Wildlife Service - Official Records

Park Regulations - Kenya Wildlife Service

CHAPTER 6   Wildlife Conservation in Conflict with Human Interests

Kenya Wildlife Service - Official Records

CHAPTER 7   Modern Tourism in Kenya

"Evolution of Tourism in East Africa (1900 - 2000)"
    by Joseph Ouma

"Tourism Market Report 1987/88"
    Ministry of Tourism and Wildlife

"Kenya In-Depth", Paper 1, 10th African Travel
Association Conference - Nairobi, May, 1985
    by D. Musila, Director of Tourism

Kenya - A Holiday Guide, by Michael Tomkinson

CHAPTER 8   The National Parks, Reserves and other Tourist Areas

A Field Guide to the National Parks of East Africa
    J. G. Williams

"Insight Guides - Kenya", APA publications

A Travel Guide and Manual, 1983/84
    Kenya Association of Tour Operators